Readers, Please Note

The story you are about to read is Mr James Vine's. The crimes he admits to, his life story and his views and opinions are entirely his own. They have no connection with Stagedoor Publishing. Therefore, we take no responsibility for anything that his life story may lead to. Mr. Vine agrees with this, and we have signed statements to this effect held at Stagedoor Publishing.

GW00536594

**I Am London's Most Successful Crook
- My amazing *true* story. I stole £10 million and never got
caught.**

by
Terry Cunningham
© 2015

First published 2015
by Stagedoor Publishing
London WC1N 3XX UK

www.zoism.co.uk

Photographs

The reproduction quality of some of the photos in this book is, we admit, not first class. In many cases they were taken many years ago, before the digital age, by amateur photographers. They have been lying forgotten in family albums or among stacks of dusty old papers. We could have left them out but decided that their potential interest far exceeds their faintness. We are sure you will agree we made the right decision.

Contents

Foreword

When asked by 'Stagedoor' to meet Mister James Vine and get his book down on the page, I had my doubts. I expected to meet a mouthy, overbearing, intimidating old gangster who I would find impossible to work with. What I found was quite the reverse - a well mannered old man - tall, thin, very well dressed, quietly spoken and with a strong London accent. He was down to earth and pleasant to deal with.

But I had to remember that he was a professional thief and there is no excuse for that. The huge amounts of money he stole - even if it was from big outfits like the Army, the Government and high class Mayfair shops - it was still money that belonged to someone else. Over the months that I worked with him, I found him to be absolutely insistent that each crime be explained in detail in relation to how it was planned and carried out. Times, dates - and as you'll see, - even photos of where the crimes took place and who with.

He was also insistent that nothing be left out, altered or glossed over, in the telling of how it all happened. It is all exactly as he told it to me. This really is one for the record books. I warned him that police regard this as the age of what they call the 'Historic Crime.' The police are arresting people - many very well known - for alleged crimes that took place over 50 years ago. James' answer to that was:

'If you follow that to its logical conclusion it means if the police see an old photo of London from the 1950's and spot my car parked too near a bus stop they will trace it's number to see who owned it at the time. Then I'll get a fine through the post for £100' 60 years after the event.'

I warned him not to joke about it because this book could very well result in him being arrested.

1

We often worked together on the book over a drink at various Soho pubs. I know Soho well myself, but Jim's knowledge of old Soho was fascinating and I think it adds an interesting historical bonus for the reader, and I enjoyed walking round the area with him.

But as the weeks progressed, he became more tired. I took him for his hospital treatment a couple of times and he seemed glad of the company, but after it he had to rest for a week or so to recover. I hope I've got the spirit of the man down on the page; I'm convinced he has been ruled by a 'danger mentality'.

Yes, he loved having big money, and living well - but I'm sure it was the sheer thrill of planning the crime and seeing if he could pull it off that was his motivation. In my work as a writer I have met many like him. They must stretch their emotions to the extreme limit. They can't live a flatline existence. They have to constantly feel the full limit of their emotions. It often destroys them.

Jim is one of those people. I hope you enjoy his story. It's certainly a very different type of crime story because it's an absolutely (and for him a dangerously) true one.

Terry Cunningham, London, 2015

Chapter 1 - The Unknown, Very Rich And Very Successful Crook

I have just got back from the hospital, made a cup of tea and I'm now 'people watching' from my window. I live in Soho, and it is (or maybe I should say was) London's most colourful, outrageous and notorious district. I'm just 5 minutes walk from Piccadilly Circus or Oxford Street. The people I'm watching are walking through Soho. And right now I would give anything to be one of those tiny people down there instead of me. But you can bet not one of those tiny moving dots would change places with me if they knew what I had been told at the hospital.

'It's cancer - no two ways about it - and by the look of this it's a nasty one', said the self important specialist holding up an x-ray film. No, I thought to myself, you're the nasty one - no compassion, no sympathy - what a way to tell someone such dreadful news! I steeled myself not to show any reaction, I refused to give him his bit of sport.

'What's to be done?' I asked as casually as I could.

'Not a lot.' came his quick and equally casual reply.

He then droned on in a boring monotone voice about major surgery, that at my age he did not think was wise, and chemo that I would find extremely harrowing.

'What' I asked once again as casually as possible 'if I refuse all treatment and take my chances?'

'Then you will die.' he replied with what I thought was a hint a pleasure in his voice.

'But don't we all do that? Can you people control the pain at the end?' This question got a one word reply.

'Hopefully.'

'How long do I have at the most?'

'Hard to say, but at the most a year or so, maybe two.'

'I'll think it over', I said like I was buying a second hand car. And with that I was gone.

As I closed his door behind me I muttered angrily under my breath 'You snot faced bastard!' And to think I was paying privately for this...should have gone with the NHS. That unpleasant meeting was what made my mind up to write this book. The prospect of death makes me very focused, uneasy, and sad, but doesn't terrify me. You look at life very differently as you approach eighty. So, with an air of *what the hell do I have to lose?* I stopped off at the supermarket and bought a stack of blank note books and several cheap biros.

The pretty girl at the check-out asked with a smile, 'Are you writing a book?' Looking at her and thinking, if only I were 45 years younger...I said

'Yes I am, well if Charles Dickens and J.K.Rowling can do it, why not me?'

'What is it about?', she asked still smiling.

'Well in a nutshell it's the life story of a crook.'

'Did he make any money?'

'Yes - a fortune.'

'Where is he now, in 'Nick?'

'No, he's free as a bird and standing in front of you paying for these books and pens.'

With that she threw back her head laughing and said 'Let me have a copy when it's finished.'

I was tempted to say something like 'Only if you come to bed with me!' but thought better of it...

Chapter 2 - A Very Different Crime Story - A True One

So you are about to read my first and last book, because I'm not a writer. I'm a criminal and professional thief (now retired) and have been most of my life. I have to say, a very successful one, I started life very poor and I am now a multi millionaire, and those millions were gained through crime. My name means nothing to you because you have never heard of me.

That is a major sign of my success and until now that's just the way I wanted it. You see if you're a famous criminal or gangster then you're a total failure. I met some famous ones but never mixed with them. Take a few world famous examples - Al Capone. Maybe the most famous crook of all time but he died in prison, so how great is that? Ron and Reg Kray lived their lives in the spotlight and everyone knew about them (including the police), and as a result they went to prison for 30 years

The Great Train Robbery - a very daring robbery, but there were too many people involved. That's why I always worked alone (or virtually so), because you're only as strong as the weakest link in the chain. That train robbery was badly planned because they left a trail of clues a mile wide and got banged up for 30 long, hellish years, a savage sentence. Clever criminals are not in prison, they are free like I am and always have been. Free to enjoy our ill gotten gains. I'm proud and pleased to say I have never been in prison, only as a visitor.

I assume my reader friend that you're reading this because you enjoy books about crime, so do I. But let me tell you from the start that this is a very different crime story. First and foremost *this is a true story*. People's names, locations, times and dates are, as to the best of my memory, correct. I do have an excellent recall memory, mainly because like most old people, I live in the past. If I do change any very slight detail you will be told as we go along. This book is also different to all others that you have read on crime because there is no sickening violence, no murders, no shoot outs, no court room dramas, and above all no long prison sentences.

It will sound to you like a contradiction in terms but in every day life I'm very honest. If I found your wallet or purse in the street then I'd hand it in at the police station. I have never stolen from the man in the street. I always hit big outfits. Modern day mugging and breaking into working class homes disgusts me. Am I trying to justify my crimes? No I make no excuses. I am slightly ashamed of my past, but the awful thing about the past is that it can't be changed. And talking of honesty, if you asked me 'would I do it all again?' the truthful answer is 'Yes,' because I hated being poor.

From where I'm standing (I'm 79) you are almost certainly a young or younger person, hence you won't recall the world, or rather London, like it was in the 1950s 60s 70s 80s. So bear with me as I describe it, and with the aid of your imagination, I'm sure you'll find it interesting and maybe realise what drastic changes have taken place in this country over the last few decades.

When I finished this book I got my hundreds of A4 pages written in long hand, typed up by a professional typist who put it on disc and sent it to several big publishers. They couldn't turn it down quick enough. Most rejection letters said in so many words; 'we like it, it's different and interesting, but not PC and sorry, too dangerous. You are admitting to these crimes that took place several years ago, but be warned that the police have long memories and almost never close a case. They will come knocking on your door, and we don't want to be involved, so thanks but no thanks.'

Then my typist told me about Stagedoor Publishing who she said were more daring and dealt in offbeat, quirky books. They said;

'we like it, it's very different. We'll publish it but it's obvious that you're not a writer - it needs a ghost writer.' I agreed, but I insisted that not one word of the story be changed. Nothing is to be glossed over or altered for the sake of Political Correctness and any royalties go to my favourite charities. They agreed and sent over professional writer Terry Cunningham. We became friends and he guided me through every page saying 'You need more detail here, this part is too short or it needs to be more descriptive there etc...' In fact he created and wrote the book.

However, he never tried to get me to change one bit of the actual story; He completely rewrote it, yet kept my story absolutely intact. He did warn me, like so many others, that I stood a good chance of the book's contents putting me behind bars. So why do It? I'll try and explain it to you. I've had my three score years and ten - plus nine - and as I've told you, my health is far from good. Also, I'm alone in the world.

All the people who meant something to me have passed on or are on the other side of the world. Every day I get up and have nowhere to go because I'm too old to travel now so cruises and plane journeys are out. Most days I walk around Soho, and weather permitting, I sit in Golden Square or Soho Square and feed the birds. Maybe once a week I get a cab down to Leicester Square and see a movie or visit one of the lovely parks on my doorstep; Hyde, Regents or Green Park. Or, take a cab over to Kensington, Knightsbridge or Chelsea but my walking is not so good now so sadly that's out. If it's possible to be in love with a city then I've had a lifelong love affair with London or, to be more precise, the West End.

I eat alone in cafes or restaurants, unless I don't feel well enough to go out. Then I cook a meal in my flat. I hate cooking, hence the meals are lousy. Then I spend hours 'people watching' from my window, reading, and dealing with the bills - gas, electric, and council tax, food, service charges and so on and so on. OK, I can afford them easily thanks to my life of crime, but I'm sick of dealing with it. I'm tired of it all.

So if it comes to paying for my crimes, what can they do to me at 79? Give me 35 years in nick? So, I'll be in a cell, but aren't I in one now? In the new one I can read, watch TV and have company. As I'm not a dangerous crook I'll be in an open prison and be allowed to walk around the local town a couple of afternoons a week with an electronic tag on my ankle.

I'll get all my meals provided and I won't have to worry about cooking, shopping, and keeping it all going - in short - I'll be taken care of. I can chill out, get my head down and wait for the end. When illness does strike hard, I'll get good medical treatment. Long before it comes to that, I'll give all my money to charity, in fact I've already started doing this. So bring it on.

Yes, I hear you say, but you could afford a luxury nursing home and still have all that without going to prison. No, I've checked out several such places and I found the atmosphere dreadful. There were wheelchairs and Zimmer frames everywhere, large communal rooms full of very old people asleep in front of non-stop trash TV, victims of the *chemical cosh* being run by bossy, sometimes nasty, nursing staff and end up on one of their end of life care plans where you're denied food and water until you conveniently die in agony.

No thanks, I'd sooner be dead. In nick there would be a mixture of interesting rogues, young and old. At least there would be lots of stimulating conversation, plus life and movement going on around me.

Chapter 3 - How It All Started

Let me take you right back in time to 1952. You're going to have to use your imagination big time because although it's within living memory it was a world totally and utterly different to today. Imagine if you can a world where if you mentioned any of the following no one would have any idea what you were talking about, these are just a few of the things that did not exist: Parking meters, traffic wardens, mobile phones (in fact only the wealthy had a landline phone), CCTV cameras, drones, the Internet or computers, Facebook, cash machines, credit cards, Political Correctness, muggers, yobs, health & safety, Rock n Roll, CDs, DVDs, Motorways, drugs and drug dealers and (maybe above all) reverse and sideways baseball caps. In it's very early form (tiny 6" B & W screens) TV sets were around, but no one I knew had one and holidays abroad were unheard of. Most of my crimes would not have been possible if some of the above had been around at that time.

OK, let me give you some background. I was 4 when World War Two started and the whole country was in turmoil. My Dad just missed being called up for army service because he was 43. He'd had me, his only child, late in life. He was an Irishman, who was very quiet, timid and reserved and he was also a very honest man with decent principles. During the war, like most working class kids, I was moved around to live with different people, mainly old aunts. I spent most of my childhood in air raid shelters and had very little schooling. I entered the working world at 14, hardly able to read or write and as for mathematics, don't go there! This also applied to the rest of my school mates, we were all in the same 'know nothing' boat.

By the early 50s the UK was a much simpler but also tougher place to be. Rationing was still in place. Even though the war had been over for 5 years food, clothing and petrol were all severely rationed. Lack of petrol wasn't a big deal because hardly any working class person owned a car. Bomb sites were everywhere, where a bomb had landed and blown up half the street and the buildings still lay in ruins.

Not knowing what to do with their illiterate son, my parents decided that I should go and work with my Dad. He was a tailor, more precisely a coat-maker, and he had a little workshop in Soho that he rented for £2 a week. Today that rent would be well over £2000. It was on the 3rd floor at 48 Beak Street. He worked as an outworker for the tailoring firms across Regent Street, in Mayfair and also Savile Row.

So that was my young life - every day, I would travel from our home in Downham (that's in the suburbs of south east London) by train to the West End. There and back would take over 3 hours out of my day and I hated it. My working day was spent making clothes with my Dad and we had a part time tailoress who helped out for a couple of days a week.

So I led a quiet life, even by the standards of the day. During my last year at school I met Mary who was the same age as me. Her parents had been killed in the war and she lived just a couple of streets away with her aunt. It was love at first sight; and like Shakespeare's Romeo & Juliet, we were just 14 years old. Very happy but also very naïve. Today's 8 year olds are more worldly and 'with it' than we were.

I did have one indirect brush with crime at that time that I think had a subconscious effect on me. A young man in his early 20's asked my Father to make him some suits. His name was Terry Hogan and he was very charming, friendly and appeared to have plenty of money. One evening, as Mary and I were leaving the workshop, he pulled up in a new MG sports car. I was always *car mad* so he showed it to me, explaining the engine and how fast it could go etc. Then he said, 'you and your girlfriend, squeeze in and I'll give you a spin.' So with Mary on my lap, we tore off round Golden Square. I can't imagine doing something like that today. No chance, 'ealth and safety and the police with the aid of CCTV would pick us up in no time. But back then as an impressionable 15 year old I regarded Terry as an exciting 'man of the world' - the sort I'd like to be, even then I thought it would be more fun to be buying expensive handmade clothes instead of making them.

Mary had got herself a job in a small tailoring factory that made swimsuits over in Eastcastle Street, just the other side of Oxford Street and about 15 minutes walk from me. Later that year in 1952 there was the biggest robbery the UK had ever known - bigger than the Great Train Robbery that took place years later in 1963. And it took place in Eastcastle Street. A mail van carrying sacks full of used banknotes from the Bank of England on the way to be pulped, was blocked in by a car full of men. Another car pulled in behind the van so it could not reverse back. About a dozen men dragged the driver and the two guards onto the pavement and beat them up; one of the gang jumped into the van and drove off followed by the two cars. It was all over in ten minutes, the van and cars were found abandoned in a side street half a mile away. They had got away with £287,000 (today's 2015 value of approximately £8 million). It was headline news for weeks and it was the talk of the nation. The police visited all the surrounding buildings including Mary's place asking if anyone had seen anything, no one had. For some unknown reason the police told the press that the hold up took place at 4am in the early hours of the morning, but it did in fact take place at 4 pm in the afternoon. No one was ever caught for the crime.

Dad still had some suits, sports jackets, and a smoking jacket for Terry to be collected, that he had already paid for. One morning he received a letter asking if he would post them to an address in the south of France. We parcelled them up and I took them over to the post office. We never saw Terry again.

Why she waited so long I don't know, but about a year later, Mary and I were walking in Hyde Park when she suddenly said 'You know the hold up in Eastcastle Street? It was that guy who gave us a spin in his MG'.

'Whatever makes you say that?' I asked.

'Well, I did see it all. My work table is right under the window looking down on the street and as the man jumped into the van to drive it away he had a scarf around his face and it slipped. All the others had masks, I'm absolutely certain it was him.'

'Have you told anyone else?' I asked.

'Not a soul.'

'Right, let's keep it that way.'

And we did.

They say Terry was involved in big crime for many years after that, he got away with it and earned the nickname *Lucky Tel*. But his luck must have run out in the end, because years later in 1995 he committed suicide by jumping from his flat window. I always remembered him as likeable and an exciting sort of guy who made a big impression on a nervous and shy 15 year old. Maybe, I thought, if I got into crime, I too would own an MG sports car?

Life drifted along quite pleasantly until I got to 18 and at that age all young men in the UK had to do National Service (that's 2 hard years in the army). Stupidly, I always assumed I'd be turned down on medical grounds because during the war I had suffered malnutrition. I was tall, but severely under weight and not very robust. Big mistake. Those lousy army doctors passed me A1.

There was a well known dodgy doctor, Dr Patel, with a practice in Kingly Street Soho at that time, in fact more than one practice. For £500 cash (today's value well over £10,000) he would write to the army saying you were suffering a severe nervous illness and were totally unfit for military service. Hence, you would never even be called for the army medical meaning you would not be wearing army boots for the next two years. Or, if you had been in the army a few weeks he could get you discharged.

Problem was I had about £5 to my name, and the very most Dad would have been able to raise would be £30. So £500 may as well have been £5 million. But many famous and wealthy men did make use of his services and so avoided two years of army service.

Many famous actors who at the time called themselves *Angry Young Men* and politicians who did lay out the £500 are still around today. Stagedoor have advised me not to mention names, so OK but I can mention a few who are now dead. Jeremy Thorpe former leader of the Liberal Party and movie Director Michael Winner, playwright Harold Pinter and Defence Minister Alan Clark.

Fingers Patel as he was known eventually got 3 years behind bars because even if an attractive woman came to see him only about a slight cold he would insist she take all her clothes off for a very, shall we say, detailed examination.

However, he never got charged for his £500 letters, because those in the know said he had written them for so many VIPs. Still, good luck to them, it's sour grapes on my part because I never had £500.

So, on a lovely April day in 1955, Mum, Dad and Mary came to see me off at Waterloo station. I was heading for Hilsea Barracks near Portsmouth to join the R.A.O.C (Royal Army Ordinance Corps).

Like all the other young men, I was in for one hell of a shock. The previous night I'd slept in my own small, poorly furnished but cosy little bedroom with my pet cat, my comics and bedside radio. The next night I found myself in a cold tin nissen hut with 19 other men who were shouting, arguing, farting, sweating and swearing. The 12 weeks basic training, which is today called 'boot camp', was hell on earth. The discipline was harsh and vicious. On average, there was a suicide every 2 weeks. I pushed open a toilet door one day to find a lad hanging there. I still wake at night seeing his awful, twisted face. We were on parade at 5am, then route marches in full pack, fire arms training (that's all day on the ranges shooting at targets), and endless parades and marches. After 12 weeks I was sent to Maryhill barracks in Glasgow for jungle training,

The UK is always at war with someone, and at that time one of our enemies was Cyprus and we were fighting the EOKE terrorists. They wanted the Brits out of their country, so that was my next stop. Once there, the strict discipline eased off a bit, and life became almost bearable, with the exception of the scorching sun. Before the army I had never fired a gun, and I have not fired one since. That's an odd admission for someone who has lived a life of crime, but as I've said, I am a criminal but not a gangster. Even so I passed out as a "1st Class Marksman" on revolvers, rifles, stengun's etc.

To my amazement I was promoted to Lance Corporal. Almost every day I would take a platoon of men to the rifle range for shooting practice. There were no ear protectors in those days, so today I'm deaf and have to wear a hearing aid - that annoys me no end. After 18 long awful months that seemed more like 18 years, I was sent home for 2 weeks leave and my Cyprus duty was over. God was I pleased to see dear old London again! I got off the train at Paddington Station and got the bus straight to Soho, Dad had now moved to another little workshop at No.6 Carnaby Street.

Next door at No.5, young John Stephen's had a small workshop. In a few years time, in the early 1960s, he would change the face of fashion forever by opening the first boutique. He made that street world famous for trendy boutiques and the very latest fashions. But this was only 1956 and Carnaby Street was just a drab little back street running parallel with mighty Regent Street. Dad, in his quiet way, was pleased to see me, getting up from the sewing machine he said: 'Let's have a drink son.' We walked round to the old workshop in Beak Street, because on the ground floor there was and still is a Pub with the strange name of *The Sun and 13 Cantons*.

Chapter 4 - The Glass Jar That Changed My Life

I called in for a drink at *The Sun and 13 Cantons* the other day. It's a small pub on a corner. The layout has been changed over the years and it's now smart and trendy with wall mirrors and plush seating. It has also been made bigger, but back then it was tiny and rather bleak. Next door, on the third floor, No. 48, our old tailoring workshop is now the office of some Media company. The same big old street door is now covered with CCTV and security locks, back then we would often leave the door unlocked all night. Funny the little things you remember. As we sat down, Dad said, 'Less than 6 months son, and you'll be home for good.'

'Yes', I replied, but 6 months is a hell of a long time when you hate every day.
'Dad' I said,' I hate to ask, but could you lend me a few quid so that I can take Mary out while I'm on leave? Because I'm almost flat broke.'

'Sure I can son' he said with that lilting Irish accent.

I knew he had little cash himself so felt mean asking him. My army wage at that time was £2.16 shillings a week and the average working man's wage then was around £12 a week. I know the army kept me, but it was still lousy money. The pub was crowded and noisy, but I pushed my way through the crowd, and when I got to the bar I saw something standing on the counter that stunned me and set my life off in a new direction forever.

A huge and heavy glass jar, standing over 3 feet tall and about 2 wide. Full to the brim with money; dozens of £5 notes - the big old white ones - £1 and ten bob ones, plus hundreds of coins, half crowns,shillings,sixpences. I heard a voice say 'would you like to win that lot?' It was the barmaid, a woman in her 40's, who seemed the bossy type.

'I sure would.'

'Well, take a card and say how much you think is in there, put your name and address and if your amount is the nearest, you get the 50 quid prize. It's taken the best part of a year to get it that full, the draw takes place next week.'

'Not much point, I'm in the army, so won't be around this part of the world.'

She winked and said 'So that's where you got the lovely sun tan?'

Then she added in too loud a voice 'Well at least put something in, it all goes to charity.' People nearby were looking, so with a smile but cursing her under my breath. I put a couple of sixpences in through the hole in the lid. Then, sexily, she leant forward and whispered 'I'll give you a tip soldier, if you make a guess, make it over a thousand'. No way was I leaving my address, so with a laugh I replied

'No thanks, with my luck it would be a waste of time'.

Dad and I finished our drinks and left. I then went over to Lambeth to see Mary, she had moved there to live with her sister in Salamanca Street in a poor little Victorian tenement flat just round the back of Lambeth Palace. Mary and I spent the next week seeing movies (or going to the pictures as we called it back then), strolling around Hyde Park and taking rowing boats out on the Serpentine.

Mary had a Jack Russell puppy called Major who came everywhere with us. It was so good to be free of army discipline for a couple of weeks. But all the time my mind was fixed on that big jar of money, I just could not stop thinking about it. Mary remarked on this, saying 'What on earth are you daydreaming about? Have you met another woman in Cyprus Jim?'

I laughed it off saying that the Cypriots hate us, we are not even allowed to leave the camp when off-duty for fear of being assassinated like some of our lads had been. In my off- duty hours in Cyprus I spent a lot of time reading - since school my reading had vastly improved and I loved reading American crime books. One guy who fascinated me was a failed actor who turned to crime, he would dress up in all sorts of disguises to carry out bank hold ups. He made a fortune but the idiot had to rob one last bank and got gunned down in the process.

His liking for disguise interested me though so I called at a theatrical costumers just off Leicester Square in Irving street called Monty Berman's, they made the clothes for all the big movies of the time. Using Dad's money, I purchased a pair of large horn-rimmed glasses (the lenses were plain glass), and several wigs with matching moustaches, even a walking stick. However, this walking stick could quickly turn into a *sword stick* should I run into trouble.

By now I had a plan forming in my mind. I remembered in our old workshop, the two windows looked out onto Beak Street. I also remembered we still had the keys to Beak Street in a drawer at our new place in Carnaby Street. Along the passage, there was a little store room that faced the back of the building. Outside its old sash cord window was a very old, rusty iron fire escape leading down to the ground and passing right by the pub's back windows. I knew now almost exactly what I was going to do. That money would set me up and alter my life completely. I had to have it.

My leave was soon over and I reported to my new army camp near Bicester, a town about 25 miles north of Oxford. The camp was a huge one set in the wide open Oxfordshire countryside and it even had its own railway system. As soon as I arrived my sergeant put me in charge of the NAAFI club (NAAFI stands for Navy Army & Air Force Institutes). It had a large lounge area, billiard rooms, a gym, TV room, plus huge cafeteria and bar. The bar could get rowdy on a Friday and Saturday night when some of the lads had a few drinks too many. It could get tough at times, and it was my job to keep order.

One of the lads working there with me on my team was Phil Gates from Stoke on Trent, a pal I'd met in Cyprus. Phil had an old American motorbike, an 'Indian' similar to a 'Harley Davidson.' I promised him £10 (3 weeks wages) if I could borrow it for the 3 days leave I still had due to me. I'd learnt to drive motor bikes, cars and trucks in Cyprus. I explained that I couldn't pay him until I got back, but being the good mate that he was he said it was OK.

So the next day I went to London again but didn't tell Mary. I had a robbery to carry out and wanted no distractions. In those days, sentences were harsh and you served the full term. If this one went wrong I knew I was facing 6 to 8 years behind bars. As a serving soldier it would be a harsh as hell military prison, probably Colchester or Shepton Mallet, well known for their vicious treatment of prisoners.

Chapter 5 - My First Crime

I parked the bike outside the Carnaby Street workshop then went round to Marshall Street swimming pool a couple of streets away. Today it's a sports centre and the pool is still there, but back then you could have an ordinary bath. I took a long relaxing one, changed into my civvies (civilian clothes) and went round to the pub. It was busy as usual but I was very pleased to see the bossy barmaid wasn't on duty.

The big jar of money was still on the counter, looking more closely this time I noticed it had a thin chain around the base and it was secured somewhere under the bar. I ordered a whisky, sat down and read my paper. As it was lunch hour, more people started coming in and it was getting very crowded. As casually as I could, I got up and walked over to the door marked *Toilets*. Once through the door I was faced with two more, one with a ladies sign and one with gents.

I pushed open the gents and slid the bolt shut behind me. I got up on the pan and took hold of the small, rusty old metal window handle. This was long before the days of double glazing. This window had probably been there since the place was built, and that, according to the sign on the wall outside, was 1882. That sign is still there today. I had to force it open and to muffle the creaking sound (I should have brought some oil with me), I pulled the old hanging chain and the water flushing sounded like Niagara Falls. I then pulled the window almost closed but left it half an inch open, I prayed that for the rest of the day no one would notice this and close it. I went back into the bar finished my drink and left.

I headed for Berwick (pronounced Be-rick) Street Market, grabbed a quick cup of tea and a sandwich, and bought a pair of black plimsolls (forerunner of today's trainers) for moving quickly and quietly, a large holdall bag, a pocket torch and small wire cutters. I then headed back to Carnaby Street, pulled the motor bike into the passage, put it on its stand and stayed in the workshop as I didn't want to risk running into anyone I knew. So I lay on the board, that's tailors speak for a work bench, and had a few hours sleep. I woke at about 10pm, it was now dark. Wearing a silver grey wig, large glasses, walking stick, black raincoat, my large holdall and Dad's old trilby hat pulled well down, I headed for my first crime scene.

There were quite a few people walking about, and I could see from across the street that the pub was still busy and crowded. I looked up carefully at number 48 next door - the ground floor was a wine company and the 1st floor was the London Shirt Co. The staff had all long gone home. The next floor was Mr Kaye's sign writing workshop, then above him, the floor I wanted. There wasn't a light to be seen, it was all quiet. With heart thumping, I crossed the street and opened the big street door, closing it very carefully behind me. I didn't dare risk the lights, so with the aid of my torch, I climbed the long flights of stairs. When I got to the top a dozen *what ifs* went through my brain - maybe the new guy has changed the locks? Maybe he is in there because he didn't bother going home tonight and decided to sleep in his workshop?, What the hell do I do if he confronts me? Fight him or make up some stupid story? What if someone comes back while I'm in there? I took some deep breaths to steady my nerves and gently turned the key... it opened.

I tip toed along to the first door and looked in. It had hardly changed, it was still a tailors workshop. Then I went along the corridor to the small storeroom, slowly lifted the old sash cord window and then came back to the workshop that looked down onto the street and the pub's main door. It was now just gone 11pm (closing time) and noisy drinkers were leaving, yelling their *goodnights* to each other. Then an old woman cleaner came out and

I could see by the street light that she emptied a bucket of dirty water in the gutter before moving off down the street.

Over an hour later the staff began to leave, I guess they'd been getting the place ready for the next day. An Austin pulled up on the other side of the road. The driver didn't get out, but a man and woman, most likely the publican and his wife, came out, banged the door shut and went over to the car. They drove off towards Regents Street. I waited another hour in case anyone had forgotten something and came back. Then back in the store room, I took off my overcoat and shoes, pulled on a black balaclava (similar to a ski mask) and my new plimsolls. I slipped the handles of the holdall over my shoulder, then out onto the fire escape and down to the pub window. Luck was with me as the window was still ajar like I'd left it.

The night was dark and cloudy and the moon mostly stayed behind the clouds. Being thin was an advantage when it came to getting through the narrow window, then out of the toilet and into the bar. I dropped to my knees to crawl across the floor and round the back of the bar. In those days policemen would slowly walk around the London streets looking in windows and trying doors to make sure all was well. The bottom half of the windows were frosted, but above that it was clear glass.

I sat on the floor for a minute or so then reached up, cut the thin wire that held it to the counter, gripped the jar and lowered it down next to me, took of the lid and tipped the contents into my holdall. I then placed the empty jar back on the bar after wiping it clean of finger prints. Fool that I was, I wasn't wearing gloves. I had to force the notes and coins down to zip the holdall shut, it was packed solid. Then listening carefully for any foot steps outside, I headed for the fire escape before getting out onto it. I looked carefully at all the windows in the back of the surrounding buildings, a few had lights on but the curtains were drawn,

In any one of those dark unlit ones, someone could have been watching me and phoning the police. There was no turning back now, back in the storeroom I changed back into my street wear. Leaving everything as I found it and no trace that anyone had been there, I gently closed the door and went back down the stairs to the street door. I opened it very slowly, half expecting a couple of big cops to be waiting for me, but all was quiet and there was no- one about.

Chapter 6 - Home And Dry, I'm On My Way

I checked my watch, it was just gone 2am. I headed up Beak Street and turned right into Carnaby. Back then Carnaby was a normal street, not closed to traffic like now. I got some stay tape from Dad's workshop. It's used in the making of a coat to strengthen the edge of a garment, it's less than half an inch wide and is very strong. I used it to bind the holdall tight and firm to the Indian's rear saddle. I wheeled the old bike back onto the road, kicked down the starter and with a screech of tyres out to Regents Street then Oxford Street, Edgware Road and on out through north London to the A41 Aylesbury Road. I kept to a steady speed so as not to draw the attention of any passing patrol car, then after nearly 3 hours I saw the "Old Iron Bridge', which is a railway bridge that spans the road a few miles before you get to Bicester. I turned left at the bridge then it was only two miles to the camp.

When soldiers got a weekend pass, they would walk that two miles from the camp to the bridge, and try to hitch a lift south to London or north to places like Liverpool or Manchester. There was an American air base nearby at Upper Heyford so if you saw an American car approaching you could bet they would stop and give you a lift as they were friendly people the Yanks. Maybe not today because like I say everything has changed. I should point out the reason for thumbing a lift was that we had no money for train fares, although in my case that was no longer true.

The next day I was still on leave as I'd got back a day early. So I gave Phil his motorbike back and instead of the £10 I promised him I gave him £20. He was delighted, and that night with some mates, he got crazy drunk in the NAAFI club. Being a Corporal I now had my own small but very sparse room in the club, what a Godsend! I locked the door and tipped the money out on the bed. I couldn't believe it; I'd never seen so much cash in my life!

When I had finally counted it all I remembered what the barmaid had said - make your guess over a thousand.'

She was right, it came to £1,404.7.8 (that's 1404 pounds,7 shillings and 8 pence in the pre-decimal money of the time). Something I always did since, but didn't do this time because I was new to crime, is check that any of the notes serial numbers ran in sequence. But like all working class people then, I had no bank account or cheque book.

Remember, this amount of money at that time would easily have bought me a nice two bedroom house in the London suburbs. Other people at the time were paying for such a house over 25 years on a mortgage. I put all the notes in blocks of £50 and sewed them inside the lining of my overcoat. I sorted all the coins into different denominations, put them into socks and tied the ends tight. I would start spending the coins first. But I couldn't spend much as I was in the army and my food, clothing and accommodation were all provided. To go out and buy a big car would look highly suspicious. Anyway, I would have to get permission to keep it on the camp and that would almost certainly be refused.

My company sergeant was a nasty bit of work, he was a regular solider aged about 45 and hated to see national servicemen get promoted, so he had it in for me. His surname was Sergeant, so behind his back the lads called him 'Sergeant Twice'. 'I've put your name down for block training, Corporal' he said with a sly smile.

This was an intensely hard 10 weeks of training out in the wilds; climbing mountains, marching all day carrying full pack plus heavy 303 rifles, swimming icy rivers fully clothed, sleeping in tents or on the ground in a sleeping bag. Then taking part in day-long mock battles with real bullets being fired at you, just a few inches above your head. NO, I thought to myself, I'm too rich for that shit! I knew this man's weakness was drink, every evening he'd be in the sergeants mess boozing. Often on muster parade at 6 am he would still be unsteady and semi- pissed after the night before, and his wife had recently dumped him.

'Sarge can I speak to you man to man? Forget the army, Sergeant, Corporal and all that. For the next ten minutes we are just two men having a chat that no one knows about outside this room'.

'Depends what's it about?' was his slow, suspicious reply.

'Money, Sarge'

'OK fire away', he said.

'What do you get a week?'
'Just under ten quid but I have to send 3 quid to the wife. Then I have to pay 30 bob off my debts.'

'OK Sarge, so you end up with about a fiver a week, that's nearly twice what a National Service Private gets.'

'Yeah but I'm a fucking regular Sergeant', he said, raising his voice to a hysterical screech.

'OK, OK calm down. How much are these debts you speak of?'

'I did owe 40 but I've got it down to just under 25, but that's taken best part of a year, what's this leading to corporal?'

'This, how would you like me to give you 25 quid right now to clear your debts, plus 5 quid on pay day every Thursday? So I clear your debts and double your wages.'

He gave a slight laugh.

'What do I have to do, shoot the CO?' (Commanding Officer)

'No, you take my name off block training and every parade including guard duty. I slip away for a 48 hour pass whenever I need it, instead of one every 8 weeks if I'm lucky. Don't worry, I won't go silly and over do it. Put my name forward for promotion, another stripe as a full corporal then I'll be even more untouchable.'

I could see he was more than interested. I slowly took a small wad of notes from my pocket, his eyes lit up.

'And here', I said, 'are 5 fivers as a sign that I'm not pissing about.'

He almost tore my hand off grabbing the money.

'Where are you getting hold of this sort of dough?'

'I have no money myself Sarge' I lied, 'but let's say someone in London is looking after me, that's why I have to go there often.'

'Right we have a deal, let me know if I can help with anything else, and I'll be breathing down your neck on pay parade this Thursday.'

With that he was gone.

I was starting to learn the power that money gives you. It confirmed what I've learnt to be true, most people have their price and in most cases that price is not very high. Just look at today's politicians. That night I checked the camp notice board and I saw my name had been taken off the list of men who had to report with full kit ready to move out for block training at 5am the next morning.

The next 5 or so months that remained of my army service passed almost pleasantly except for one slight hitch. Sarge said that the officer at the medical centre, a 2nd Lieutenant Peter Hill of the RAMC (Royal Army Medical Corps) wanted to know why Lance Corporal Vine should be promoted to full Corporal because when he called for a kit inspection he was never present, always on leave, and for a crack shot was never seen on the ranges.

'I think he will cause trouble if he smells a rat' said Sarge with a sigh.'

'What do you know about him Sarge?'

'Nice bloke, the men like him, he's an old Etonian who trained as a Doctor before the army but failed the last exam. He comes from a long line of Generals and Colonels. Loves the ladies and horses but backs a lot of losers - that's ladies and horses.' Sarge gave one of his very rare grins. 'He's run up big bills at the Officer's Mess (the Mess is a sort of club where military personnel socialise). His Dad bought him an expensive Alvis car that he's trying to sell to pay the bills. He's car mad as well. One good thing about him is that he is approachable. Do you want me to see if we can buy him off?'

'Yeah Sarge, sounds like he has some expensive past times and as a result he will be in need of money, and if he digs deep enough we'll both be on a court martial. See if you can fix a meeting but tread very, I do mean very, careful.'

Old Sarge did well because the next day the officer called at the NAAFI club to see me. A man in his 30's, smart looking but he seemed ill at ease.

He then said 'I know what you're up to and it won't be long before other ranks start to notice.'

'OK Sir, what do you suggest?'

He laughed, so I knew we could do business.

'You have a mock accident.'

'I'm not prepared to shoot my foot off!'

'No, you fall heavily on the concrete path, get carried up to my medical centre and I put you off all duties for at least 4 months or until you get demobbed.'

'Sounds good, the very most I can go to is £250.' (I would have gone much higher.)

He looked slightly shocked but also very interested.

'I would try to get you a discharge and a pension but for that we would have to involve other officers, so too risky.'
I counted out £250 and as he took it he gave a huge sigh of relief saying 'this will get me out of some deep shit.'

'Glad to hear it.' I told him. I considered it money well spent.

I did as he asked and a couple of soldiers found me lying on the floor outside one of the nissen huts one rainy evening. 'I've just gone arse over head lads. I think I've broken my hip, can't move, I'm in fucking agony.' I said it whilst shaking and speaking through clenched teeth, and over acting like mad.

'Hang on Corporal.' They got some other lads who were passing and carried me up to the medical centre where Lt Hill did a great job. He put my leg in a splint, gave me a walking stick and a chit saying I was excused all duties pending X-Rays until further notice. No one was going to question that. I sent Mum and Dad

£150 and Mary £200. Told them a silly story about winning £350 in a big raffle at the camp. They wrote back saying thank you and how fantastically lucky I was. Well, I believe you make your own luck.

Mary also mentioned that she was pregnant and that news frightened the life out of me; twenty and I was going to be a Dad. We had to marry of course, because to be an unmarried mum in the1950's was the equivalent of being a war criminal. Single mothers were treated appallingly. That's something that has changed for the better. I took a 48 hour pass and with me riding pillion and Phil driving (he had offered to be my best man) we headed for London on the old Indian motorbike. Mary and I got married in the Catford registry office, and then had a meal in a nearby cafe for only a dozen or so guests. I had to make out I couldn't afford a big church wedding. There was a bit of truth in this as my money was down to less than half what it was when I left the Soho Pub that night.

Many years later I was best man at both of Phil's weddings. He died far too young aged 36, he was a great pal and I still miss him.

My demob day finally arrived in April 1957. I was free again and determined to get involved in crime, and above all to make it pay. I still read at least two or three true life crime books a month; they had to be real factual stories as I had no interest in fiction.

Most of the crimes were exciting and interesting to read about, but for me were too dangerous. Things like bank robbery or breaking into a building where you knew a safe full of money was waiting, but then you would need the combination, or a blow torch, and of course you would have to involve many other people, so for me that was a non-starter. Like with my pub job, I was determined to try and be a lone wolf. I'm too old now of course, but if I were in crime today, I would get into internet or cyber-crime; the possibilities would be endless and international.

THE £200,000 LONDON MAIL-VAN ROBBERY: THE SCENE AND THE CLUES.

INJURED MEN
WERE
FOUND HERE

BANDIT CAR
ESCAPED UP
ONE-WAY STREET

MAIL VAN
CAME
THIS WAY

BANDIT CAR
PULLED ACROSS,
AND BLOCKED ROAD

The scene of the Eastcastle Street Mail Van Robbery that took place on May 21st 1952. Mary (later my wife) witnessed the robbery from the window of her firm and saw that one of the gang was Terry Hogan. We told no one. They got away with well over £200,000 (the police reported £200,000 but it was nearer £300,000), today's 2015 value is approximately £8 million.

48 Beak Street, Soho. Where it all started, as it is today. It hasn't changed at all from when I worked there in the early 1950s. Beak Street runs directly on to Regent Street.

Scene of my first crime - *the glass jar full of money* - from the pub counter. I entered via the large blue door on the right, number 48.

48 Beak Street, from where I was able to enter the pub next door via the fire escape. Today it's covered in security locks but in my day was often left open 24 - 7.

Me ready to leave to do my first robbery at the pub in Beak Street
- on Phil's American Motorbike, the *Indian*.

Army Nissen Huts - each one housed 20 men.

View of the main road in Bicester Army Camp HQ Company,
pay office on the right.

The camp NAAFI club at Bicester. Packed with soldiers spending money every night.

The Globe, the camp cinema, showing three different films a
week, an absolute gold mine.

As a Corporal I had my own sparse room, as opposed to sleeping in one of the Nissen huts with twenty other men. I was able to count the money from the pub job in private.

Lieutenant Peter Hill leading his men on parade. He masterminded the robbery at Bicester Army Camp and we got away with
a fortune. A great guy.

The 1949 Humber Hawk that I used as the Colonel's staff car.

My old place on busy Newburgh Street in the heart of Soho as it is today. Teresa lived above the shop. The present day shop *Peckham Rye* has no connection with this book.

My beloved 1939 Chrysler Kew that Laura and her East End mob
used for a smash and grab job in Chelsea.

Soho's busy Berwick market where I sold 8,000 shirts stolen from
Stoke-on-Trent.

The end of another busy day in Berwick Market.

Theo's two sons cleaning up the market after another busy day.
The same sons who unloaded over 8,000 shirts on my return
from Stoke-on-Trent. I was always putting odd jobs their way;
they would turn their hand to anything and ended up running a
successful café.

Chapter 7 - Home Again In Soho, London

On my return to Soho and tailoring I heard about an old tailor who was retiring, he had a nice workshop in Newburgh Street, right in the heart of Soho. It was nicely laid out, he had all the latest equipment, it was ground floor and had an extra smaller room plus bathroom. This would do as a flatlet if I worked late and wanted to stay the night. The rent was a reasonable £4 a week so I took it.

Dad came to work with me and we worked for three firms in Mayfair and one in Savile Row. In those days we got around £6 for making a jacket or £9 for an overcoat, smoking jacket, dinner jacket etc. A present-day tailor tells me they get around £600 for making a coat – but it's still hard work and just average money. We could do about 4 a week. It was hard work, long hours and the work was focused and very intense. It was piece-work, so no sick pay, holiday pay, overtime or pension. At the end of the week we ended up with just a bit more than an unskilled worker. Also the scene was changing, casual clothes were getting popular and work was getting a bit scarce. To cap it all, lots of Cypriot and Hungarian tailors were coming over, so it became a *two men chasing one job* situation.

Dad, with his dry Irish sense of humour said "You should have shot all the tailors when you were over there." I could also see Dad was getting old bless him and slowing down and the journey up to town and back each day was telling on him. Mary and I rented a dreary old flat in Lambeth near her sister.

That sister phoned me one afternoon at work to say I was the father of twin girls. I sat at the old Singer sewing machine, stunned but also delighted. I rushed over to Lambeth to see my lovely daughters Kim and Debbie, quite trendy names for the time. Back then it was all Floss, Gladys, Elsie and Iris, we named them after two film stars of the time; Kim Novak and Debbie Reynolds.

Soho was full of life back then, It was known as London's *Casbah*. The busy lively markets, hundreds of little cafés, interesting small shops, clubs, gambling dens, strip clubs, clip joints, pubs and at night prostitutes would lurk in doorways. But none of these dodgy people would bother you; you could go about your business in safety.

Berwick market was total entertainment. It couldn't exist today as political correctness and health and safety would shut it down within minutes. Big stalls with four wheels and a tent- like roof, lined both sides of the street selling everything you could think of. Men would just open a suit case on the pavement and start selling items from the case like watches, and cheap jewellery. The good hearted banter between sellers and customers was pure music hall comedy.

My favourite was *Tosh the Tie King*. Tosh was a friendly term of London greeting like Pal or Mate, you could greet someone with 'Hiya Tosh, how you doing?' I never knew his real name but the whole of Soho knew him. On his stall he sold ties, shirts, socks, silk scarves and gloves. He had a permanent crowd around him eager to buy. If he saw a classy looking gent walking by, he'd stop him saying in his broad cockney accent: 'Blimey Guv-nor come 'ere, what's that bit of old rubbish round your neck?'

The shocked business man would protest saying 'What the devil do you mean?'

Tosh would then go into his routine. 'Come ear!!' With that, he would as quick as lightning take off the man's perfectly good neck tie and replace it with one of his own.

Tosh's ties were very loud, as was the fashion of the time. They were hand painted with pictures of Big Ben, skyscrapers, naked women, wolves, etc. 'There you go Guv, with my compliments, nothing to pay, just tell your high class pals you got it from Tosh the Tie King.' The man would move off red- faced and protesting like mad. By now his audience would be in hysterics and move around the stall waving money, eager to buy, what a salesman!

I was chatting to him one day when he mentioned he was packing it all in because of heart trouble. He said it was a tough job in the winter, out in all weather. On the spur of the moment I said; 'how much for the business Tosh? That's the site fee licence for the place in the market, all the stock and the stall?'

'£75 to you, young man and you'll make a fortune.'

An hour later I was selling ties and enjoying myself. It was good to be out in the air. I had recently got myself a small car, a 10 year old Standard 9. It was so handy for driving over to the East End to get stock and of course to and from Lambeth. Dad decided to retire and do some work from home. I did tailoring 3 days a week and the market 3 days. In the fine weather the market paid very well but when it rained trade was dead. I had about £400 left from my pub job, but as for money coming in, I was just about keeping my head above water.

Chapter 8 - I Go North To Get Into The Shirt Business

Phil, who was by now out of the army, came down from Stoke for a long weekend with Amy his wife. We all went to see a show at the Palladium and dined out a couple of times. While Amy stayed in with Mary and the girls, I took Phil to see the workshop and my stall in the market. He was now working as a warehouseman and told me about a plan he had for a *big job* worth a lot of money. He had never done any sort of crime and it would be a once-only thing on his part and I was the only guy he would trust - plus the fact that I had the means of moving the loot, so was I interested? Yes I was, but with reservations. I always wanted to work alone. That's not always possible of course, but one other person is my limit and that one I must feel absolutely sure about.

This was the set up. He had been working the night-shift at this place almost a year. It was a huge warehouse just outside Stoke in a place called Hanley. Just about everything you can think of except food was stored there. It came straight from the Liverpool docks and stayed at this place, sometimes for weeks at a time. All types of clothing, furniture, car parts, you name it. At any one time, four or five large trucks, the sort that today you see doing house removals were parked in the car park packed full of various items. For example, one would be packed with mirrors, another with raincoats, but they never carried a mixed load. When they pulled out they delivered to shops, garages and department stores. There were no supermarkets back then. They went mainly to the northern cities and north Wales, never London.

One truck every few weeks was packed with shirts - 8,000 of them. He had brought one down to show me, that he would replace as soon as he got back. It was white, long sleeved with a smart button down collar, twin pockets and made of very good quality cotton, silk material. I was impressed as I knew a quality garment when I saw one. They came in Medium and Large sizes. That was a plus because Small and Extra Large are hard sizes to move. I knew without checking that they would sell in Regent Street's *Austin Reed* or *Jaeger* stores for around £15 to £20, even in those days (today around £100 to £130). It came packed in a clear cellophane envelope and best of all there was no makers label in the neck. When I asked Phil about this he said the stores put their own special label in with their name and logo.

'OK, so Phil how do I get my hands on them?'

'You come up and drive the truck out of the yard, six hours later you'll be back in London. Simple as that, they may not even miss it for a day. The security is non-existent except for burglar alarms, but that's only if you break into the building. The place is run on a shoe string.'

'Phil it isn't that easy, what about ignition keys to the truck?'

'Yeah, I've written this down; it's the key number of the truck. It's a Bedford; you get the key down here'

'Before we go any further Phil, the police will say *Inside Job* before they finish their tea.'

'Let them prove it, if it comes to the crunch I'll confess. I'll put my hands up and say 'I was sleeping, so sack me', it's their own fault - if you pay peanuts, you get monkeys and monkeys are notorious thieves! You're not laughing Jim?'

'No Phil, it's too serious for that. What does Amy know about this?'

'Nothing and she never will.'

'Have you even hinted this to anyone in Stoke?'

'Not a word.'

'The police will be very suspicious of you, the bastards can be vicious, and they might try and beat it out of you.'

He stubbed out his fag and said 'after two hard years in the army I can stand up to them.'

'When will the next truck load be ready?' I asked.

Phil looked pleased that I was interested and said 'In six days. Next Thursday it will be packed and standing there with a full tank of petrol ready to roll, the driver will call for it at 8am Friday morning.'

'What sort of cut were you thinking of?' I asked.

'I leave that entirely up to you and you don't give me a penny until you've sold them.'

'How will you explain to your wife suddenly having a lot of extra money?'

'She won't ever know anything about it; she doesn't even know what I earn now, come to that', he laughed 'What will you tell Mary when you start wearing a new shirt every day? You know our trouble Jim? We like women, maybe too much, but we don't trust them.' We both laughed.

'OK Phil let me think about it carefully.' When I dropped them off at Euston station to go back to Stoke, Phil shook my hand, almost breaking my fingers.

He was a powerfully-built strong guy, and said with a smile, 'You take care my old pal', then gave me a friendly wink. For the next two days I had that adrenalin rush I get when I knew I was on to something.

A couple of doors along from my workshop was an old Greek shoe repair man called Theo who lived above the shop with his two sons who were always ducking and diving, doing anything to make a few quid. They worked at cleaning up the market after the working day was over. I called round to see them. 'How would you like £20 each, an extremely good week's wages, for a few hours work?' At once I had their full undivided attention. 'I'm getting a large delivery of shirts; they're arriving by a big truck. It will park up outside my place at 5 or 6 in the morning and I want it unloaded as fast as possible, you'll have to work flat out until it's empty. I will park half on the pavement but will still almost block this little narrow street, so I've got to have it gone long before 7 when the traffic starts.'

'Sure Mister Vine, no problem, just ring our bell and we will be down the stairs two at a time.' I had done my homework and knew I could sell these shirts for £3 each as bankrupt stock. If there are approximately 8,000, that's £24,000 over say a year, even minus expenses and Phil's cut, I'll get 8 or 9 grand out of it minimum. I couldn't believe it. Sure there was a risk but not a massive one. It would be a northern crime and would not make any waves in London until they found the truck.

I planned to dump that as quickly as possible. The biggest risk was that they would suspect Phil but I had full faith in him to hold out. The other risk was that just round the corner in Broadwick Street was Trenchard House, a police section house, where young unmarried police lived. It would only need one of them to be returning there late and see the truck being unloaded in the early hours. He would almost certainly check it out and within a few minutes I'd be in handcuffs. But the money outweighed the risk, so I said to myself...Let's go!

First I ordered labels to go in the neck of the shirts; they were peel-off stick on silk, with the words "Royal Shirt Co. Burlington Arcade. Mayfair. London. W1, with a logo of a gold crown, very flash. Needless to say, there was no such shirt Co. Then I called on a guy I knew in Lex garage just round the corner who got me the keys to the truck for £5. Of course he had no idea what they were going to be used for.

Phil had sent me a stolen driving licence belonging to someone in Burslem, a suburb of Stoke. He had bought that from a guy in a pub ages ago. Back then the licences did not have your photo. It was starting to take shape. Thursday, I got the train to Stoke wearing old jeans, lumber jacket and cap with my large horn rimmed fake glasses, I hadn't shaved for 3 day's. I carried nothing, no ID except the driving licence and about £10 in cash. From Stoke on Trent mainline station I got a bus to near the warehouse, then from a phone box, phoned and let it ring six times. Phil knew I was outside waiting in the dark on a bus stop. He turned off the lights, then on again several times, meaning 'come over it's clear.' He let me in a side door. The place was huge like a hangar for a jumbo jet, stacked with goods of every description.

Phil explained that the driver's route and delivery instructions were in the glove compartment and he had painstakingly typed out a false one on headed company paper of the places I was going, all in London and the South, somewhere these trucks never normally went to. He even matched up the driver's name with the one on the licence - a bit OTT I thought at the time. But, it proved to be great thinking. There were four trucks parked in the compound. On their sides was the name of the truck rental Co, not the warehouse. The big gates were open, lax even for those days. Phil said he had checked our one and it was packed with 8,320 of those shirts.

The truck keys fitted perfectly, the big old beast started first time and we rumbled out of the yard. Phil had even drawn me a map of how to get out of the area quickly as there were no motorways back then. So I had an early version of a sat-nav pinned on the dash to help me onto the London road. I was on my way, I couldn't believe it was this easy, the roads were almost empty. It was a dull night with slight rain. Dear old Phil had made me a sandwich that I had on the seat beside me and took a bite of now and then. I'd found my way onto the right road for London and had been driving for over an hour when I noticed a motorbike in my wing mirror. It had been there for a while, not trying to overtake me and all I could make out was the single headlight. I slowed slightly to make it overtake, it did, and my headlights lit up a police patrol bike. They rode Triumph 500's back then. He gave a stop signal telling me to pull over.

Oh Christ, what the fuck is this all about? My mouth went dry with fear, and the butterflies in my guts felt more like eagles. We've overlooked something; they were just waiting for us to drive into a trap. No point in making a run for it, I don't even know where I am. He put his bike on its stand and came over to my door, he looked the officious type. 'Turn off the engine, driver', he snapped.

I dropped into lovable but stupid truck driver mode, complete with silly grin, saying 'Don't tell me I was speeding? This old bus won't do more than 50 flat out, and going uphill, well you may as well get out and push...and..'

He cut off my comic banter with 'What are you carrying?' I thought 'For Christ's sake crawl.'

'Shirts, Officer. For all the big shops in London.'

'Let's see your papers.'

I got Phil's worksheet that he'd typed for me and handed it down to him. 'Driving licence!' he snapped again, I handed that down as well. 'Open up, I want to take a look.'

'Sure', I said, jumping down to the ground, he still hadn't given any reason for stopping me, what the hell was it all about? I opened one of the huge doors.

'Bloody hell, how many are there?'

'Not sure.' I said 'But when I get back tomorrow night, I'll be knackered after unloading them.'

'OK, close up', then he started kicking the trucks tyres and looking all round it. I thought to myself *this one's out to find anything he can to nick me, but he doesn't realise it's stolen thank God.* I started to breath normally again.

Suddenly we heard a crash and the sound of breaking glass, his bike had come off its stand and fallen over. The gods were with me. 'No, no!' he yelled. 'Its sodding brand new.'

I now dropped into the roll of lovable helpful truck driver 'Jump in, I'll drop you at your police station.'

'No, I must stay with the bike.' He was calling up help from the radio attached to the bike's tank. I heard them tell him that a van was coming out to him to pick him and the bike up. He had lost interest in me completely; he was trying to straighten out the bike's bent handlebars. 'Get on your way driver.'

'Sure I can't be of any help officer?' The relief was making me over confident - a bit longer and I would have given him a free shirt to cheer him up!

That smashed bike will keep him occupied for a while, but what the hell made him stop me anyway? I wondered. I guess it was just a routine check. I bet he thought he could nick me for a couple of things because the truck did look old and shabby. He never made a note of the name on the licence and he didn't look very closely at the places I was going to deliver to. Still, the sooner I get off these open roads and deep into London streets the better.

So I put my foot flat to the floor, the old Bedford shook, groaned, and rattled. At times going downhill we even hit 55mph. It was dull and dark at just after 6am as I pulled into Soho. I opened up the back, the two lads were ready and we started to unload flat out. In my place all three rooms were packed almost floor to ceiling with shirts. I jumped in and drove the old Bedford up to Euston station thinking that if I parked there it may lead the police to think the driver had gone back to Stoke by train. So, I parked the old Bedford in the street alongside the station then jogged back to my place.

Later that morning I gave the old lady on the top floor the first 500 shirts and a reel of the flash labels. I forget how much, but I paid her well to stick them in. She was very poor and delighted with the extra money. I put a huge notice on the stall saying... "BANKRUPT STOCK MAYFAIR. SHIRTS USUAL PRICE £20 EACH. MY PRICE £6 FOR TWO. ONCE ONLY OFFER. VERY FEW LEFT". They started to sell like hot cakes, so I opened another stall in East Lane market, that's a couple or so miles away across the river Thames in South London. Mary's sister ran it for me. In less than four months they had all sold. After taking out all the expenses including Phil's cut, I was left with around £9,000.

Now you, as a fan of crime books may think stealing shirts is not as exciting as, for example, bank robbery. Well this is why I am free to spend my millions and most bank robbers are in prison.

To rob a bank takes a minimum of 3 people who are usually already known to the police. If you have to shoot your way out, the crime can turn from robbery to murder, and in those days for murder you were executed (hung). Even if the bank job is successful, very seldom did each share at that time come to £9,000.

The police did not seem to suspect Phil; he broke down and confessed to having a sleep in the tea room and did not see or hear the truck going. All the trucks were there when he checked the yard at 1am; the police took no further action. The firm did sack Phil though for sleeping on duty. Phil was renting a little 'two up two down' house in Carlton road five minutes walk from Stoke on Trent station, his parents had lived there before him. The landlord later gave him the offer as a sitting tenant to buy it for £500. He sent me all the papers and I bought it for him. When the shirts were almost sold out he came down to see me and I gave him £8000 in cash. That's equivalent in 2015 to over £200,000. Or put another way 8 grand can buy today what £350 would back in the early 1960's.

As a cover, he took a job as of all things, a bank messenger for about a year, and then started to go slightly mad. He would suddenly take off for New York, Paris, or Spain for expensive holidays. His marriage hit the rocks and he got involved with a 17-year old girl. They got married and it lasted about six months. He told everyone including wives that he'd had a big win on the football pools, they were the forerunner of today's lottery. He bought several fancy cars, mainly Jags.

On his last visit he was driving yet another one 'What do yer think of her Corporal?' he laughed as he pulled up outside my place. I told him, it was a step up from the old Indian motorbike we shared. We had a great few days around town calling at strip clubs, pubs and generally having a laugh.

'You're going through your money too fast, Phil'

'I know, Jim, we've got to do another job.' There was a hint of desperation in his voice and he had a plan to rob the bank where he last worked. But the plan was by no means foolproof, so I said a definite no. As I said before he died at 36 of heart trouble. I went to see him in North Staffs hospital. We talked about our army days and the shirt job. 'You turned my life around Jim, if it weren't for you I'd still be working my arse off on night shift in that lousy warehouse.'

He gave a weak laugh and said; 'here, I've got you a present.' It was a khaki T-Shirt with the words *Hilsea Survivors Club* written on the front. Though not at the same time as me, he had been through the hard as hell training camp at Hilsea.

'Have you got much money left Phil?'

'No, I've fucked, drank and driven my way through the lot' he laughed, then added, 'and when I'm taken out of here in a box, I don't have the price of a funeral.'

'If it comes to that mate, I'll take care of it.' I told him, and I did. 'Why not move down to London and I'll give you a job?'

'No, my roots go deep in dear old Stoke, same as you in London Jim.'

'Well, think about it old pal.'

Then taking my hand in his still strong grip he said,' I will corporal, and thanks for everything.'

He died later that week. I often wonder if he would have been happier without ever doing the shirt job.

Chapter 9 - I Meet The So Called Big Time Criminals

My own marriage was starting to stall; Mary seemed to want nothing more than hanging around Lambeth gossiping with the neighbours. We both adored the girls of course and tried for another child, hoping for a boy, but it never happened. I shut down the tailoring and with the money from shirts I moved into other things, I started a firm called *Soho Cars* with my pal Len, who worked in Lex garage in Brewer Street - it was a petrol station and car repairs then, now it's the same building but has turned into a NCP multi storey car park. Len could get cars cheap, maybe they had some very slight damage. I would buy them, get them put right and put them up for sale. I would simply park them in or around Carnaby Street with a big 'For Sale' sign in the window and a great write up about the car.

Carnaby was starting to get very busy with hundreds of people visiting all the boutiques, so the car would sell in a matter of days. If the car was an upmarket model I would park it over in Mayfair, in or around Bond Street. I remember I got a pre-war model Lagonda, paid £700, parked it in Bond Street and sold it the next day to an American tourist for £2,750. He had it shipped back to the States. This was not an illegal business but it was crime money that got it started.

I got involved at this time with Laura; she was a barmaid at the Lyceum in the Strand. It's a theatre now but back then it was a dance hall. I don't like dancing, but I did like Laura. She was a Jane Mansfield lookalike and it was a highly sexual relationship; in other words, I couldn't keep my hands off her. She was an East End woman and knew several of the well known gangsters from there. I never told her anything about my crimes; all she knew was that I was a car dealer. We went clubbing and through her I met the Kray Twins.

I'll be honest, I found them dull. They had no humour and were very suspious of you until they knew who you were in case you were a *grass* (a police informer). They just regarded me as Laura's guy, a car dealer. I had to be careful because they disliked people from south London or 'over the river' as they called it. But all they and their crowd talked about were crimes, some very violent ones. All their conversations consisted of was 'What did Frank get for that jewellery job?'

'Oh he got 7 years and the rest got 4 each.'

'What about Jock and Mac with that dog racing scam?'

'Yeah they got banged up for 6.'

The Krays were not the top of London's underworld as people think. They were controlled by a highly intelligent ruthless crook, an older man called Billy Hill and his gypsy wife known to one and all as Gyp. It was he who masterminded the Eastcastle Street mail van robbery, and legend has it that Gyp drove one of the getaway cars. Via Laura I met this mastermind a couple of times. Billy Hill was into everything; he controlled casinos, clubs, racetracks he had a West End penthouse and a villa in Spain. The Krays and every other crook in London did nothing without Hill's say so. But for all that he spent 17 years of his life behind bars. So once again I ask, how successful is that?

At that time I owned an American car that I adored, a1939 Chrysler Kew; it had been laid up on blocks during the war and had done less than 3000 miles. It was like driving a WW2 tank with turbo, what today they would call a big muscle auto. These day's big heavy cars are common place in the UK like the Range Rover, but not so much back then. So, my big heavy beast was ideal for what Laura's friends had in mind. I would often take Mary and the girls for a run to Brighton in it at the weekend. The girls called it our Al Capone car.

One evening Laura phoned and told me to leave the keys in the ignition and the car would be stolen, but I'd get it back in a few days plus a couple of hundred quid, but not to report it stolen until she said so. I didn't like this one bit but what could I do? The sort of crowd we were now running with, you didn't say no to, or if you did you could expect trouble big time, plus a severe beating. I didn't trust any of them, including Laura, so the next night to cover myself, I did report it stolen. Just as well, because a day or so later, they had welded a heavy iron girder across the front grill and used it for a smash and grab raid on a small but highly expensive jewellery shop in Kings Road Chelsea in broad daylight.

The four man gang drove across the pavement at full speed, slammed into the glass shop front, the driver stayed behind the wheel. The gunman stood out on the street firing warning shots in the air to frighten off any would-be heroes. The other two calmly loaded tray upon tray of watches and jewellery into sacks. They went into the shop and beat up the two terrified staff, locked them in a back room and loaded up more gems from the counters.

A small police patrol car, I think a Ford Anglia, was first on the scene and tried to block the robbers in. The gang's driver sounded the horn, the other three piled into the Chrysler, then reversing fast, smashed the small police car on its side and badly injured the police officer. A member of the public stupidly gave chase but his car was no match for the heavy beast Chrysler that ran him off the road, and he was also badly injured. The upshot of it all was that they got clean away with the robbery.

Laura did not phone until after the raid, so I would have been in deep shit if I hadn't already reported it stolen. My beloved car was a wreck, smashed windows, dents and scrapes along both sides, so I had it broken up for spares. I got the insurance money but I didn't want it, I wanted my car. I never got the money Laura promised, instead I got an expensive watch courtesy of the Kings Road. I never wore it and gave it to a friend.

At this point I knew I had to get away from these people, clean away. One friend of Laura's was Tony Costello, who latched on to me big time and was always borrowing small sums of money. One night the police knocked on my door asking 'Can you confirm Costello was with you here all yesterday working on one of your cars as he claims he was?' I was cornered and I admit scared.

'Yes' I said 'he was here, I give him part time work.'

The police knew I was lying, I felt sick. It turned out he was involved in a wages snatch. But with my alibi he got off. Ronnie Kray phoned me the next day to say 'Reg and me want to thank you for looking after our Tony, if anyone ever gets heavy with you. Come and see me and they will be dealt with very severely and hurt bad.'

Tony's next job was with three others robbing a Post Office. They got away after knocking the guy behind the counter senseless, they all carried guns and a member of the public who tried to save the Post Office money got shot in the leg.

They got well away. Tony and one of the others were sitting on the back seat of the speeding get away car tearing open the packs of money and started throwing the wrapping paper out of the car window. A passing police car saw this and tried to pull them over to tell them not to litter the streets. When the idiots saw the police car they tried to out-run it. So a long, high speed car chase followed, ended with a smash, and they were arrested.

They were put on remand in Brixton prison. Laura phoned to tell me all this and ask if I would take her and Tony's wife to see him in prison as they wanted to fix up a good mouthpiece (lawyer) to take his case. So, I took them. I'd never been in a prison before and it had a chilling effect on me as it was so depressing. Huge doors slamming with heavy bolts sliding shut, prisons back then were hellish. We spoke to him through a thick glass window, with brutal looking warders everywhere. This, I thought to myself, is not clever crime, it's plain life-wasting stupidity. He went away for 11 years in some prison way up north, so visiting him for his wife and kids was out of the question.

There is nothing more dangerous to the professional criminal than *A Woman Scorned* - many a clever crook is behind bars today because he cheated on a lady who knew too much about him. So I was delighted when Laura dumped me for a south London gangster called Richard Hart who later got shot dead by the notorious *Mad Frankie Fraser* at the *Mr Smith Club* gang fight in Catford, South East London in 1966. It also gave me the chance to cut loose from her possessive grip and to get free of the crowd that we were mixing with.

That was as close as I ever got to so- called real criminals and gangsters. To be honest, I regarded them as idiots. Some made a lot of money but wasted it all or had to pay big-time for protection and to be set up with false identities and spent many years either in prison or on the run. Most of the small time or average ones would have been better off in a run of the mill ordinary job. Once I got clear I never again had any dealings with those people that I regarded as totally stupid losers.

Chapter 10 - I Move Into The Property Business, My Own And Other People's

The chance came my way to buy where I lived at 11a Newburgh Street, a little street running parallel with Carnaby Street. My workshop that was on the ground floor, I had now turned it into a flat come office. Occupying the floor above was an Indian family, whilst on the top floor was the old lady who did my shirt labels and had lived there for years. With three sitting tenants, I got it for £3,000. I paid cash and it left me near broke but I now had the rents coming in, plus the *Soho Cars* money, and of course owning my property outright, my credit rating was excellent. I shut the stalls down when the shirts ran out so I was ticking over. I sent the girls to a little private school near where they lived. They loved it, and I saw that Mary wanted for nothing, but to my massive regret I couldn't get her to leave Lambeth and join me in Soho.

My next caper came in the form of a tailors *Trotter* - let me explain, it's a nick- name that dates back hundreds of years. A Trotter is (or was) a 'general dogsbody', a 'tea boy' a 'go for'. When the cutter has cut the suit, the Trotter would take it from Mayfair over to Soho to the tailor and bring finished garments back, then go and get the cloth and the trimmings. It was a hard job because you were on your feet all day, walking back and forth around the West End day in, day out in all weathers. Worst of all it was very poorly paid. All that makes for a bitter and resentful Trotter.

The one that came my way was a Scot named James Minty, known to one and all as 'Jock Minty.' He came from the Bellshill area of Glasgow but had been in London since before the war. He was now well over seventy and living in a dirty little, desperately poor, run down tenement block called "City of Westminster Dwellings". It was in Marshall Street, the next street to me. It's still there today but it's been smartened up a bit since Jock's day.

He had been sacked for being too old and slow to do the work anymore. I'd known him slightly for years and would often see him playing darts with his old pals in a pub I called into sometimes and would buy them a quick one. He always had his wife with him, who was blind, and I thought it touching the way he told her all that was going on around her in the pub.

I just regarded him as a nice pleasant old guy. I'd not seen him for a couple of months when he called late one night at my place looking very down. He told me his wife had died suddenly, he was now alone, and wanted to return to Glasgow where he had a brother. In the big suitcase he carried he had about six suit lengths (a length is about three and a half yards, enough for a two piece suit). I could see they were very expensive materials. He told me he took them one at a time from the last firm he had worked for - 'Huntsman's' in Savile Row - in revenge for the way they had treated him. I could tell he was bitter and felt a lot of resentment. He was taking a chance on me, I could have picked up the phone to the police, but as you will know by now, that's not my style.

He was desperate for money. 'I have no pension,' he said with a long sigh, 'I don't even have the fare back to Scotland.' He looked crestfallen and sad. So I bought them. I was no longer in tailoring but I still had connections, one of them was Doug Hayward. He was a guy about my age at the time that had his own business. Later he would make clothes for and became pals with Michael Caine, Terence Stamp, Kirk Douglas, and many other big movie stars of the time, and he opened a shop in Mount Street, Mayfair.

The next day I phoned Doug and he came over and bought the lot, making me a nice profit for just handing the cloth over. I like deals like that. A couple of nights later Jock was back and he

68

wanted to talk; maybe he had used the cloth deal to test me, sort of putting his toe in the water. What he had to tell me in a nut shell was this - over the past twenty five years he had worked for several top Savile Row tailors - two in particular were *Anderson and Sheppard* in Savile Row and *Cyril Castle* in Sackville Street.

He had made copies of the keys to these places. He knew the best day to strike when the wages for all the staff, all the outworkers, plus the money for the cloth firms would be there in cash, and they had not changed their routine in decades. He knew the layout of the premises down to the last detail; he had even carefully drawn maps to follow once inside.

'OK Jock, why haven't you done the job yourself before now? Why do you need me?'

'Because I'd be a number one suspect, and I've waited too long' he said sadly. 'Time has passed me by, I've got old and lost my nerve. if I ever had any.'

'As you say Jock, it would point directly to you.'

He gave a long sigh, then slowly said 'But not if I'd been in Glasgow for a couple of months when it happened.... surely?'

'Look Jock', I said. 'If we hit both places, they will be looking for someone who worked in both places, and that's you Pal. They will work out that you set the job up then handed it over to someone, and that's someone's Me.!'

'I'd never grass on you ……'

'Maybe not on purpose Jock, but they're clever, they could trick you.'

'No, no, look, spare me half an hour and I'll show you' he said jumping up and heading for the door. We got in a car outside that I had for sale, and we drove round to Savile Row. There on the corner was *Anderson and Sheppard*, a large old corner building they opened in 1906 and closed in 2006 when that corner was pulled down. Today you can find them in the next street near Burlington Arcade. The big double doors on the corner were the main entrance, but along on the left was an unassuming single door. Me and Jock sat in the car parked two hundred yards away in Clifford Street, where we had a clear view of A & S.

The third Thursday in every month was *The Big Day*. All the money was there waiting to be paid out on the Friday, explained Jock. Everybody would be gone by eight, even the cleaners, so I let myself in. I climb the stairs facing me, through the second door on the left was a small office. There was a big wall safe over on the left-hand wall, and of course Jock had the combination. I was thinking that my disguise would be good - grey wig and glasses - an old man working late. If I let myself in at around 10pm, I'd be out by 10.45, walking slowly away with my walking stick and heavy case.

'How much do you reckon Jock?'

'They only pay out once a month, so it's a minimum of £8000 because there will also be builders money there too. They have a couple of dozen builders working out the back on a new back entrance.'

'Ok, let's look at job number two.'

I drove to Sackville Street, which was just a couple of streets away. We pulled in and I cut the engine and lights. It was an elegant, large, glass fronted shop called *Cyril Castle Tailors*. But this was different...this guy Cyril lived above the shop in a luxury flat with a well-known pop singer of the time called 'Yana'

70

(pronounced Yar-ner). He also mixed with a showbiz crowd, so people could be calling at all times - tricky!

The time to hit the place would be any second or fourth Wednesday in the month, because he pays out every other Thursday. Jock added that he is not as big as A&S but there would be a minimum of £3,000. Remember, my reader friend, for that money then, you could buy a very nice 3 bedroom detached house in an upmarket London suburb. He also has rolls of the most expensive cloths that money can buy, lying in the window. I thought to myself, I can move them the next day via Doug Hayward and he won't even ask where they came from, although of course I'll let him know they're hot.

'OK' I said, 'I will have to study the whole thing in much more detail Jock, but I can see right now that the major problem is you. The police will jump on anyone who worked in both places and had access to the keys, and much more than likely, there isn't anyone else who worked in both those firms. Right now, all I can think of is only do A & S and forget Castle.'

But that, I thought to myself, would be letting the cloth sales to Doug Hayward of around two grand, slip through my greedy fingers. I also thought about old Jock taking off for Glasgow with several grand in his pocket, who a week before didn't have the price of a packet of fags until he collected his old age pension. No, too risky, I could do it as I would enjoy the thrill and the challenge, but there would be too many come backs. Yet the thought of all that money still nagged me.

I still had my dog old Major the Jack Russell; Mary found him a bit of a pest, so I took him on. He was a great pal, sitting with me all day in the office and he loved going out in the car. Every day, I'd take him to one of the parks, usually Regents Park or Hyde Park. He would tear round the Serpentine and then for no reason at all, charge into the water and out again, while I lay on the grass.

It was in one of these relaxing interludes that it came to me. Yes, *Yes*, I had a plan, the two robberies could be done.

Chapter 11 - Jock Goes Home In Style

I called round to see Jock. 'OK, this is the deal; the two jobs are interesting and have potential. My sixth-sense tells me that we can trust each other and you have gone into great detail with all that you've told me, so I will buy the jobs off you. But you must go back to Scotland at once and I will pay you now, then I may or may not do the jobs at some future date. If I don't, then it's down to me and that's my loss. Tomorrow, we go to my bank and we tell the manager who I know well, that I am your nephew and I am helping you return home for your final days. You have £2000 in cash which is your life's savings that you keep under the bed (a lot of people did that back then, a poor working class man never set foot in a bank). So, you put the money in a bank account and you will get a cheque book and I'll show you how to use it. On top of that, I will give you £100 in cash that will get you home and settled in style, then you're set up for life, how's that?'

He looked at me dazed and then started to cry. I made us both a cup of tea, then explained to him that he had handed me two jobs on a plate. I would do them several weeks or months apart, and if the police did check on him, he already had his money when he came to Scotland ages ago. The money couldn't be the proceeds of a robbery that took place a couple of days ago, or even if they think it could, it would be very hard to prove.

At the bank, the manager was taken in by Jock's poor, humble, old man act.

The day after that, a lovely summers one, I put him on the train home. As the train pulled out, he waved with a huge smile and shouted 'let me know how it goes Jim.'

Sure, I'll send a postcard either from Monte Carlo or Wormwood Scrubs. I put it all on ice for about five months and got on with selling cars and spending time with Mary and the girls. As it got close to Christmas, I planned the *Cyril Castle* job. It was dark by just after 4 o'clock and the West End streets were full of Christmas shoppers, so ideal working conditions.

Then I did something you may think a bit odd, but in actual fact it was actually a clever touch. I visited the shop one afternoon and, once inside, I took a good look at the layout. I made a mental note of doors, locks, everything. It was a big place with large mirrors around the walls and lots of dark mahogany tables with rolls of the most expensive cloth's on - the best silk mohair that money can buy - crombie, cashmere and vicuna.

While I was browsing, Richard Todd the film star came in, and Castle came out of the fitting room to greet him and explained that he was with Roger Moore right now trying on some suits, and would he care for a drink while he was waiting?

A few years later he would make all the clothes that Roger Moore wore in the James Bond films. This guy was at the top of the tailoring tree, he would later be known as Frank Sinatra's tailor or *The Showbiz Tailor*. I purchased a classy, expensive silk tie and left. A suit would have cost me around £90 to £120, but bear in mind that at that time you could get a good off-the-peg one for £15. Castle's were hand-made and beautifully cut. The place screamed of money and I sensed that Jock's estimate of the job being worth a minimum of £3000, was way too low. I decided to strike on the Wednesday before Xmas.

I carefully dressed the part in a long, dark overcoat, white wig with homburg hat, horn-rimmed glasses and walking stick. The reflection in my mirror told me that I was an elegant, old gentleman aged around 70, who carried a very large black leather holdall. I parked one of my for-sale cars in nearby Cork Street. There was a phone-box at the top of Sackville Street from where I could see the shop, so I phoned the number and it rang and rang with no reply. Jock had told me that after working hours, calls would be switched from the downstairs shop to Castle's flat above. So it's now or never. There were a few people about, but only those hurrying for their train or bus after a late night out. I approached the main door, the keys worked perfectly and I was in. I closed the door gently behind me

I was then faced with an unlocked, glass door that led into the front shop, and a tradesmen's passageway on the right, that led through to the small back office, and a flight of narrow stairs that led up to the flat. I had studied Jock's map and details until I knew them by heart and it was all just like he said. I opened the heavy, metal cabinet and there in two deep drawers were packs of envelopes bulging with cash. Each one had a name of a person on the front, or a company. There were also packs of cheques that I ignored, I worked with the aid of a tiny torch and in no time the cash was in my bag. Then I tip toed, bending almost double, so as not to be seen from the street up to the front of the shop where I had seen all those incredibly expensive lengths of cloth. I was forcing the last one down into my huge bag and closing the two straps, when my blood turned to ice.

There were loud voices at the main door and a key was being turned in the lock. I froze. All along the front of the mahogany counters, there were curtains. I slid one back and got under, crouching with my knees up to my chin in the dark alongside boxes of paper patterns. I hardly dared breathe. The loud voice was a man talking to a woman and they sounded slightly pissed. He kept trying the key in the lock and then it dawned on me. Oh shit, stupid sod that I am, I closed the door behind me but didn't lock it. He was trying to unlock it and then he pushed the door open. 'What the hell! The bloody door's open, it wasn't locked!' he shouted.

'Are you sure Claude?'

The woman sounded worried.

'Of course I am, it's that dozy George who's forgotten to lock it.'

Jock had told me all the names of the staff. Claude was Cyril's brother who worked with him, and George Playford was a salesman.

'You wait here and I'll check just in case there is someone in there.'

'No Claude, call the police and let them check.'

'What, for an unlocked door? Don't be silly!'

With that, the lights went on, and as he passed my counter I saw his shoes. I can still see them - highly polished, black leather. Would he pull back all the curtains to look under the counters? Would he not see that most of the cloth from the front window counter was gone? Then I heard him running up the stairs to check the flat. While he was there I could make a run for it, but the woman was waiting in the street for his return. OK, I could push her aside.... all she would see was a white haired, old man in a long overcoat with a big bag, but that heavy bag that I could hardly lift, would slow me down. OK, leave the bag...I can't do that, as there's enough in it to buy property, it would take a working man 20 years to save that much.

All these insane arguments were going back and forth in my head while I waited for this Claude to pull back the curtain and see this young man made up to look old crouching like a frightened rabbit. I heard him coming back along the passage. 'It's alright darling. All's well, you know the lovely French clock that Cyril got at Harrods for Yana's Christmas present? Well it's still on the office table, all gleaming gold and silver, that's the first thing any burglar would have taken.'

Not me Claude! I thought to myself. I had seen the clock, but items that have to be sold on at a tenth of their value and can always be traced back to you, are of no interest to me. All that does interest me is cash, and the one exception in this case is the cloth that I can turn into cash the next day via Doug Hayward. The lights went out and the couple went upstairs, still talking loudly and laughing. They'd obviously been out for the night, having a good time.

I sat motionless for at least an hour or more until the faint sound of their voices stopped. Then I came out from my hiding place and stood still, listening intently for the slightest sound. Then like a soldier defusing a bomb, I put the key in the lock and slowly and gently, opened the main door and closed and locked it behind me. I waited in the large porch, looking up and down the street, and then as an old man would, I walked slowly back towards Cork Street where my car was waiting. I drove away from Mayfair and circled Piccadilly Circus a couple of times, checking my rear-view mirror to make sure that I wasn't being followed.

Back at the flat, I dropped the heavy bag on my bed, got out of my disguise and took a shower. I felt very tense and annoyed with myself for not locking the door - a mistake that could have ended very badly, if not tragically. It was now close on 3am but I stayed up for the rest of the night counting the money, it was over £5500. At 9am I phoned Doug, told him I had something very interesting to show him and I'm giving him first refusal but I have to move it today. He was at my place 30 minutes later, and when he saw the materials his eyes lit up with excitement. He saw the names of world-famous cloth firms printed along the edge of the cloth; *James Hare, Dormeuil, Hunt & Winterbotham* and *Holland & Sherry*.

'It's all red hot Doug, so be careful.'

'How many people did you have to murder to get your hands on this lot? And where did you get it, Buckingham Palace?'

He asked the question like he was dreaming. Needless to say, I didn't answer. He was a down-to-earth, working-class bloke with a quick sense of humour. They say Michael Caine based his character on Doug in the film *Alfie*. People like him were very fashionable in the 1960's, especially with the upper classes. He even went on holiday to the Caribbean with Princess Margaret, but as time went on he got a bit too self-important and put on an upper-class accent.

He knew the cloth was worth well over £3,000 so when I said 'give me fifteen-hundred,' he came back with the cash an hour later. I had to laugh when I thought of all his world-famous customers - Royalty, Movie Stars, and Politicians - wearing clothes made of stolen material! So that made my total from the Castle job around £7,000 - less Jock's £2,100 – it was a very nice final wage of around £4,900. Bear in mind that at that time you could buy a brand new Ford car for under £350. And I still had the Anderson & Sheppard job to do.

But that turned out to be a non-event. I can't explain it even to myself, but my sixth-sense told me not to try it, maybe my close shave at Castle's had shaken my confidence? Thanks to Jock, I had it laid out on a plate. All I had to do was walk in and collect all that money. Maybe it was just too easy... so I let it go.

Beware, there are a lot of cowboys in the West End nowadays, turning out rubbish tailoring at sky-high-prices who give the trade a bad name. They are not tailors, with them you'll be paying top dollar for mediocre tailoring. Any fool can cut round a paper pattern and no doubt they're clever salesman, but I challenge them to go in the workshop, put on a thimble and sew a garment together and construct it by hand. They may as well call themselves airline pilots when they can't fly a plane. If you're going to buy custom-made clothes, go to the small one-man band firms, that way you won't be paying for the massive Mayfair overheads. Or, try the very high end off-the-peg.

Right now, some idiot is trying to re launch the Cyril Castle brand. I'd say forget it, he was great in the '60's but styles change. Today he wouldn't stand a chance, and it's much the same with crime. If you tried the *look at me I'm a well known gangster* style like the Krays did back in the 60s you'd get wiped out within a week.

London crime now is controlled by sinister foreign gangs who stay in the shadows. They're fast-moving, highly technical, dangerous and totally ruthless. Our police have their hands tied by political correctness. So, for the most part, are powerless to stop them. They deal mainly in people- trafficking and drugs. There are fortunes to be made, but they're welcome to it. Definitely not my scene.

Chapter 12 - I Take On The British Army And Win

Sitting in my small office late one evening, there was a faint knock on my door. There stood a tall, smiling guy that I knew but couldn't place. 'How's things Corporal?' he asked as we shook hands.

'Well I'll be!...Lieutenant Hill?'

'Right first time' he said with a laugh, then added 'call me Peter, and it's Captain now, if you don't mind!' still laughing. 'I'm staying in London so thought I'd look you up. I asked around for Jimmy Vine the tailor and someone pointed me in this direction'.

'No' I said, 'I packed that in years ago, I'm in general business now. You're still in the army?'

'Yes, back at Bicester after spells in other camps, and a year in Kenya fighting the Mau Mau terrorists. Took a couple of bullets in my leg.' He pulled up his trouser leg to show a nasty, deep scar. 'And a spell in Malaya and came back with Malaria! It's a bastard of an illness to live with, so maybe I'll be lucky and get a medical discharge at some future date, might even get a small pension. My dear old Father went bust before he died so I'll come out to the hard working world. The thought of working in a factory from 8 till 6 scares the hell out of me more than any terrorist with a Sten gun.'

'I know the feeling Peter, come on I'll treat you to a meal, we've got some catching up to do.'

'Not if you don't mind Old Sport, I'd like to discuss something with you in private where we can't be overheard, I take it you're alone here?' he said looking around the room.

'Yes I am, so take your coat off, get comfortable and go ahead.' I poured a couple of drinks and we moved over to the arm chairs. After some light-hearted catching up, he started on what he had really come to see me about.

'We have worked together before so I know I can trust you, and if you're not interested I know it will stay with you alone. And if it's not for you then I'll forget the whole thing because there is no one else who could pull it off with me' he said leaning forward in his chair. His voice and manner were deadly serious, like he was explaining to his men a plan of attack that involved crossing a minefield.

'Before you go into detail, just tell me, is it robbery?' I asked.

'Yes, just about the biggest you ever dreamed of' he replied, finishing his drink.

'As you're still in the Army does it involve the Army?'

'Yes, one hundred percent.' He spoke in a slow, deliberate way as though choosing his words carefully. He had become a serious man whereas I remembered him as jokey and easy going guy with no trace of snobbery, most unusual because all Officers in those days were very snobbish, thinking they were superior.

'Once again, before you go into detail, another question. When we pulled that scam when I was a Corporal at Bicester there were three of us, don't forget old 'Cross-my-palm-with-silver-Sergeant-Twice.' He almost laughed at my description but settled for a slight smile instead. 'Because if we pull an army job, he will remember us and come out of the woodwork, so we'll have to include him'.

'Not around any more Jimmy, killed in an accident in Germany where he was posted about a year after you departed. He was demonstrating grenades when a faulty one blew up in his hand killing him and two other soldiers outright.'

'Shit, I'm sorry to hear that, he was a bit of a sad sort of bloke, I don't think he ever got over his wife dumping him.'

'No Jimmy, it was drink that finished him, even before the grenade.'

We both fell silent; I broke the silence by asking 'Another drink?'

'No, I want to keep a clear head, could I have a tea?'

'Sure, I'll join you in that. Sugar?'

'Two please.'

As I made the tea, I knew instinctively that what he had in mind was big and therefore dangerous, I wasn't rich but comfortably off, would my greed for money get me in way over my head, and why did he need me? I trusted him, he had matured since I last saw him and he'd seen action in Malaya and was a cool customer with a steady nerve.

'OK Peter, will this involve anyone getting badly hurt or even killed, or put another way, will guns be used if it came to a shoot out? If the answer is yes, then don't say any more, because I'm out before you start.'

He answered me quickly, 'Sure I agree with you, the answer is no, absolutely no guns or violence of any sort. The only people who could get hurt are the two involved, me and you. And the sort of hurt would be going to prison for a very long time. I have to tell you there is a fair chance of that, but on the plus side the rewards are enormous.'

While he lit a cigarette, I lent my head back on the armchair, closed my eyes and thought hard. If the pay-off is as big as he thinks, then I'll make it my last job and live well and in style. The rest of my life will be free of any money worries, something most people strive all their lives for. I took a mouthful of tea, my favourite drink, and said 'Yes, tell me all about it, but be warned, I may still say thanks but no thanks.'

He nodded and said 'Sure, that's ok by me because if it's a no from you then it's finished, I do no more about it.'

He then, slowly and calmly, laid out the most incredible plan. In many ways it was too simple by far. If an outside criminal gang had been listening to him, they would have said 'You can't be serious; you're having a laugh surely?' But I knew the RAOC Bicester Army Camp Depot very well and I began to realise it was possible. Totally insane, extremely dangerous, no way-out if caught, only defence to plead guilty, but still possible. To put you in the picture, let me explain the camp to you as it was in those days.

I left the army in 1957 and it was now nearly 1962, just before the end of National Service. At that time Bicester was the biggest army depot in the UK, it was huge and wide open, set in the middle of the Oxfordshire countryside. This was no army camp with a wall around it. It covered more than 12 square miles, had its own railway system with 60 miles of track that connected up with the rest of the UK rail network plus sidings, level crossings, and a couple of small stations and over 30 miles of road. There were close on 25,000 soldiers and about 2,000 civilian workers who came in every day from Oxford, Aylesbury and the town of Bicester.

The depots were enormous, open buildings, big enough to house several jumbo jets. They were packed with absolutely everything the army needs from a hand gun to a tank, plus clothing, fire-arms, ammunitions, trucks, half-tracks, motor bikes. You name it. The men were divided up into A, B and C Company. Then the smaller HQ Company that consisted of a NAAFI club, the Globe Cinema, the armoury and shooting ranges, the guard dog section with 100 dogs plus kennels, a valet service, massive cookhouse, the camp barbers, the medical unit complete with small operating theatre, and the pay office. It was this last location that was of the utmost interest to me and Peter. Terrorism was something that happened in other countries, mainland attacks by the IRA or Islamic terrorists were unheard of, so security was lax.

Once you turned off the A41 main road by the iron railway bridge and drove along a small road for 2 miles, you came to the entrance. There were other entrances but all much the same. There was a single-bar barrier across the road with one, or at times two soldiers on duty, who might very rarely ask who you were. But mostly the barrier would be in the raised position and they would wave you through, as they would visitors, buses, taxis, and the coaches that brought in the civilian workers every day. Once in you could lose yourself for days. The flat, grass landscape was dotted with hundreds of nissen huts. They had a curved, corrugated iron roof with brick ends and a door. Each one housed 20 men with 10 beds down each side.

This was Peter's plan; I'll try and explain it as simply as I can. Pay day (or pay parade) was every Thursday. There would be 8 or more officers sitting behind a long table with long lines of men facing each one. When it came to your turn, you had to step up smartly, salute, then state your name, rank and number. He would then hand you your wage in a folded envelope with a staple through the notes, plus some change. You then stepped back smartly saying 'Money all present and correct Sir,' salute, about turn and march off. You didn't know if it was correct until you checked it once you got outside. It always was, but it was all a load of army bullshit, hence payday took all day.

There were other pay parades taking place at the same time in other parts of the camp but it was the HQ one that we were very interested in. The money for that was delivered to the company office the night before in 3 very large thick black leather holdall-type cases with padlocks and a huge W.D. (War Department) stamped on the side. They also held the takings from the *Globe*, the camp cinema, the NAAFI club, valet service and the bar takings from the Officers' and the Sergeants' mess.

Then on top of all that was the soldiers wages, and there must have been well over 4,000 of them in HQ. It was very hard to say how much money would be ours if we pulled it off, but Peter's educated guess was in excess of £75,000 (today's 2015 approximate value close to £760,000) and according to Peter, who had done his research meticulously, over 80% of it was in cash.

Peter and I both sat quietly for some time, me thinking of all the massive *ifs and buts*. Then he said in his gentle, high class voice, as he got up from his chair; 'I'll leave it with you Old Sport and give you a ring in a few days. You can let me know if it's yes or no. Don't worry I'll phone from a phone box in Oxford. I'll never use an army phone, and of course I'll be very guarded in what I say.'

'No need,' I said. 'My answer is yes, let's go for it, give me 10 days and I'll have it all ready to go at this end. But we must have a meet to go through it in detail before we strike.'

'Carpe Diem, Carpe Diem' he said with a smile.

'What the hell does that mean?' I asked.

'It's Latin old sport, it means *Seize the Day* and that's what we must do, seize the day with no thought or fear of tomorrow.'

Then we shook hands and he was gone. With that, I fell back in my chair and said aloud to myself 'Holy shit! What have you let yourself in for this time, you maniac?'

His audacious plan was based on fear and massive amounts of bluff. The vast majority of soldiers at the camp were young, 18 year old national service men who had just come from 16 weeks harsh and vicious basic training camps (boot camps) like the 'Hilsea Barracks' camp in Portsmouth where I had been. The discipline was hellish. They had been trained to regard an officer as God. At the sight of one, you sprang to attention, staring straight ahead and saluted. Officers spoke in a high, public school, penetrating and commanding voice, and the Privates mumbled in uneducated obedience. Watch any old British war movie from the 40's or 50's and you'll see what I mean. Today of course it's all changed, but back then the UK was a different planet.

Every two or three weeks a young soldier would have to do Guard duty. This would be from 6pm through to 6am. Usually there were 6 Privates, 1 Corporal and an Officer, as a rule not a rank higher than Captain. You would patrol whatever it was you were guarding - the cookhouse, the armoury, or in our case, the pay office. Depending on the Officer in charge, 2 men at a time could have a rest inside the building while 4 patrolled. They would all be armed with 303 rifles, half way through the night the *Tea Wagon* (a mobile canteen) would arrive and the lads could have a welcome *cuppa*.

In all my two years of guard duty nothing ever happened. Maybe once in a while a senior officer, usually a Major, would drop by in a staff car, inspect the men who would be lined up outside, then ask the duty guard Officer 'Everything alright old chap?'   He would reply 'all's well Sir, nothing to report.' The guard - strange as it may seem - was not specifically to protect the money, because there could be a guard duty at the pay office on another night when there was no money present.

The plan can be explained fairly simply, but the attention to detail required, timing, and complexity of carrying it out was terrifying. I would be a Lieutenant Colonel and drive down from London in an army type car, arriving around 2am. I would call at one of the nissen huts where Peter knew they were drivers and very new recruits. I would demand a driver as my chap had been taken ill, because a Lieutenant Colonel would never be driving himself.

Peter would be in the throws of a Malaria attack - a good excuse for not knowing what he was doing. He said he could bring on an attack by simply not taking his tablets for a few days. He would get a phone call from me to say there had been a stupid cock-up and they had delivered A.B & C Companies money to HQ by mistake and a senior officer was on his way to collect it, and replace it with the correct HQ money. I would arrive by staff car with army driver, wearing the uniform of a Lt Colonel. I would have 3 identical cases stamped with the words *WD HQ Company*. They would be stuffed full with old newspapers and telephone directories.

I would be playing the part of a high-ranking officer and over-acting like mad, talking in a loud, commanding voice and giving orders all-round. I would be very concerned about Captain Hill. Peter would be in a hell of a state- sweating, shaking, incoherent - half an act and half genuine. I would pretend to phone the medical centre to come and get him, then tell my driver 'I have a better idea, take Capt Hill's car and get him to the medical centre now, don't wait for them as they have to come 4 miles to get here.'

Meanwhile, I will drop these bags off at the guard room, they can get them over to A.B and C Company, then I'll get back here and take over the guard. The guardroom was on the left of the entrance as you come in opposite the Globe cinema. I would then drive the car out of the camp and back to London as fast as I could. By the time all the mayhem had settled and they realised I was not coming back, I should have almost reached London by the time the shit hit the fan and all hell would break loose. My part for now would be over; the spotlight would be on Peter, would he be able to take the intense heat? Come to that, would I? Would anyone?

Chapter 13 - I Get Promoted To The Rank Of Colonel

First, I needed the uniform of a Lt. Col (Lieutenant Colonel). I purchased the correct material and made it myself, complete with 2 pips and 1 crown on the shoulder epaulettes and red tags on the collar. I got an Officer's hat from Berman's and put a red band around that. As I looked in my long mirror I thought *Yes, you're starting to look the part.* Then I started to grow a neat military style moustache. Next, the car; nearly all army staff cars at that time were Humbers in brown or khaki. I got the latest Exchange & Mart that always had a big car sales section,. I couldn't use my contacts in the car trade because there must be no way it could be traced back to me. Try as I might I couldn't find the exact car I wanted but came up very close with an ex-army Humber Hawk. It was in excellent condition, as an ex-army vehicle would have been maintained regardless of cost.

It was a light tan colour with a dark brown roof, column change, sun roof and wind-out windscreen. A large, roomy, comfortable car that was around 12 years old. That was no problem because the army then were still using motor transport from the last '39 - '45 war. A young guy down in Bromley was selling it for £125 as he found it too heavy on petrol. I paid him cash, gave a false name and address and drove away back to Soho.

It may sound odd, but every night in my flat I would dress up as a Lt.Col and practice my Officer's voice and behaviours - giving out orders and commands, coupled with arrogant mannerisms – in front of my long bedroom mirror. I also made up a pendant in the R.A.O.C colours on my trusty Singer sewing machine, to go on the outside wing of the Humber, plus a square plate to be fixed to the front bumper with the large letters OFFICER STAFF CAR. W.D HQ BICESTER.

I got a call late one Monday evening from Peter who was just a few streets away in a call box. 'OK to come round Jimmy?' I told him I was alone and it was.

'If you're up for it Old Sport, it's this Thursday' he said calmly as he pulled the arm chair nearer the fire, and put the three empty cases with WD markings on the floor.

'I'm ready to go', I told him, I hope, equally calmly. I then gave him a full dress rehearsal and wore the uniform – horn-rimmed glasses, (I'd decided against a wig so had a very short haircut), and used theatrical gel to add ageing silver to my hair and moustache, and of course the voice.

He was pleased but added some valid points. The crease in your trousers must be sharper, that watch is not the sort an officer would wear - too flashy, and don't wear any rings. Otherwise, great. He then went into great detail as to how we were going to carry it out, including plan B, a fall-back plan should it go wrong. And a plan C if we were caught red handed. He talked for over an hour covering everything in minute detail. I told him about the Humber that was parked two streets away with a full tank ready to roll. He was currently driving, for him, a rather mundane Austin A40. 'After we pull this, don't go out and buy a Bentley, Peter, it would look highly suspicious.'

'No chance Old Sport, those days are over.' I hoped he meant it.

Phil's dying gift to me. I never wear T-Shirts I'm a collar and tie
man, but I've kept it all these years and wouldn't part with it.

This is my trusty walking stick that, with a pull on the handle, can be turned into a sword stick. I bought it back in 1958 to take on my first crime job at the pub. In case it went wrong I could at least try and threaten my way out.

Sword sticks were very common from Victorian times right up to the 1960s. A large shop on Charing Cross Road sold nothing but sword sticks of various designs. Just as well I never had to use it, I would almost certainly have stuck it through my own foot. They are now classed as illegal.

The two seats in Soho Square where Peter and I met after the
Army Camp robbery to discuss our new wealth and both being
Rolls Royce owners. The two pigeons taking off in the photo are
probably ancestors of the ones I feed most days now in my lonely
but financially secure old age.

Three prostitutes standing in Macclesfield Street, leading down to
Gerrard Street that is now China town. They are waiting for
customers as they did on most Soho streets. It became such an
embarrassing nuisance that the Government brought in the
'Street Offences Act' in 1959 that made it illegal to sell sex on the
streets.

Cyril Castle, who's Mayfair shop I robbed, seen here fitting a jacket on film star Roger Moore, to be worn in his next *James Bond* movie. Castle was known as the *Showbiz Tailor* throughout the 50s and 60s. His girlfriend, Yana, along with her showbiz friends brought him a lot of trade. However, it was when Frank Sinatra became a customer that all the big American stars also wanted their clothes from Castle. Sinatra was so pleased with his stage suits that he invited Castle out to his home in Palm Springs for a couple of holidays.

However, by the mid 70s a lot of his fickle showbiz customers dropped him for my dodgy stolen cloth buying friend Doug Hayward who by now had a shop in Mayfair. That, plus an ageing clientele and massive rent hikes meant he ended up in a back room in Conduit Street making just a couple of suits a week for old regular customers. Like so many of the Mayfair and Soho people I came across over the years whatever did they do with the big money when it was rolling in? I guess the answer is they spent or rather squandered it.

Yana (pronounced Yar-ner) was a very glamorous British TV, stage, and recording star of the 1950s and 60s. She was also Cyril Castle's live-in girlfriend in his luxury flat above the high class tailors shop in Sackville Street Mayfair.

She had a great love of animals and kept as many as three poodles and at one time a pet monkey in the flat. Rumour has it she dumped Cyril to go to the States and appear on US TV with movie star comic Bob Hope (who some say she had an affair with). Sadly, she died in London in 1989 aged 57; she made big money in her day but must have spent it because her last job was serving in *Boots* the chemist, and demonstrating slimming machines in Harrods.

It was the very expensive gold French clock that Cyril had bought her for Christmas that saved my neck when I was robbing the shop.

The *White Horse* pub, run in the 60s and 70s by my friend, ex-cop
Walter Sandison.

11A, the street door that caused so much trouble.

Number 11A Newburgh Street. My house that French call girl
Teresa forced me to sell to her at a massive loss. The shop above
was, in my day, my workshop. *Peckham Rye* has no connection
with this book.

Teresa, as she appeared in all the contact magazines.

SuperBitch magazine, that I managed and Susan Land owned,
selling 10,000 copies a month.

The mysterious but clever Susan Land, editor and owner of
SuperBitch magazine. Photo taken at the rooftop open air *Oasis*
swimming pool, Covent Garden.

RAM Books, in Old Compton Street. Run by tough front man Cliff Freasy but owned by John Humphreys. He had 40 branches in Soho alone.

John Humphreys and his wife Rusty in their Dean Street flat. They ran over 40 sexy book shops in Soho and had the West End police in their pocket. In the mid 70s his shops were making over £100,000 a week. I have to say I found them a charming and very pleasant couple to do business with.

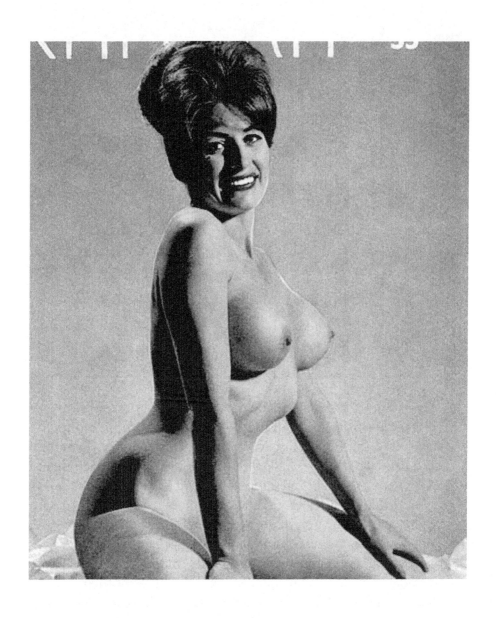

John Humphreys' wife Rusty in her stripper days. Her stage
name was Rusty Gaynor (real name June Packard). She later
proved to be a clever business woman.

My daughter, who had just passed her driving test, with my
vintage Rolls Royce. Out of all the things my crime money
brought me I think this car gave me the most pleasure. I bought it
in the late 1960s for £3,250, a hell of a lot of money back then,
and owned it for over twenty years. I always kept it as a second
car and had another car for daily use. It was a 1929 or 30 model
with a 4 litre straight eight engine and semi automatic gear box.
Top speed was only around 70 mph, but what luxurious deep
leather seats, with large arm rests, vanity mirrors in the back for
the ladies plus a cocktail cabinet that my girls kept their Coca
Cola in. Plus small pull down satin wood tables and a wind up
glass division that would separate those in the back from the
driver. The girls would use this when they wanted to talk about
their boyfriends without Dad hearing.

My longest journey was London to Torquay and back; it never let me down and never needed any major work. When running it was almost silent and had a lovely elevated driving position. When driving it I would often think; *yes crime can and does pay but only if you work almost alone and keep a low profile* (apart from one's choice of car that is!)

Soho's Old Compton Street in the early 1960s; full of life,
restaurants, pubs, cafes, clubs and at least 4 or 5 of John
Humphrey's sexy bookshops. His main one *Ram Books* was at the
far end of this photo on the right (the Charing Cross road end).
That shop alone sold around a hundred a day of Susan Land's
magazines. Today the street has the nick name *The Gay Highway*
because of all the Gay bars and clubs there

Chapter 14 - Right This Is It, Ready To Go

Thursday arrived and I had a lay-in, spent the day quietly and then slowly started to get ready. As midnight approached, no call had come from Peter to say it's off so I got dressed in full uniform but with a dark raincoat covering it all and also a trilby hat. The Colonel's hat was in my holdall, along with the car's pendant and badges. Once clear of London, I pulled into a quiet lay-by, fixed the pendant and WD badges to the bumper, put my raincoat in the boot and changed hats. Two hours later I turned left at the Iron Bridge. It was a dark night and bad nerves kicked in when I saw and remembered the huge arc lights lighting up the depots in the distance. I realised I was sweating slightly and my hands had a slight tremble, maybe I was getting too old for all this, but there was no turning back now.

As I turned by the Globe cinema, to my utter relief, the road barrier was in the *up* position, with one Private soldier on gate-duty stamping his feet and clapping his hands to keep warm. On seeing the staff car he sprang to attention and saluted. He stood out in the moonlight because of his white belt and gaiters as he was a regimental policeman. They were similar to the military police (the dreaded 'Red Cap's') - but they have jurisdiction everywhere that troops are; regimental only have powers within the camp.

I acknowledged him as I drove through by casually touching the brim of my cap with my gloved hand as officers did. I checked the clock on the dashboard and it was 2.35 am. Almost a mile down the road, I pulled up outside the nissen hut that Peter had instructed me to. The lights were on and loud voices with Liverpool accents were arguing about something. I flung the door wide open, the lads were obviously up all night getting their kit ready for a parade - shining boots, polishing belts and buttons and cleaning rifles.

A Corporal shaving in a small mirror fixed to the door of his metal locker, looked stunned. His expression screamed 'What the fucking hell is a Colonel doing here at this time of night?' 'Atten-shun' he yelled, and the men in various states of undress stood stock still staring straight ahead. The hut was now in total silence. Now it was time for Lt Col Maitland, that was the name Peter had given me, to kick in like never before. '

Stand easy gentlemen' I commanded. 'Corporal, we have an emergency. I need a driver, my chap has had an accident, can you supply one immediately?'

'Ye..Ye..Yes sir I'm a driver, 1st class.'

'Splendid, good man, get dressed and be outside in five minutes flat.'
With that, I got into the back seat of the Humber, and about four minutes later, the Lance Corporal came running out of the hut still doing up his tunic, and jumped in behind the wheel.

'Do you know HQ company office?' I asked.

'Yes Sir.'

'Right, that's our first stop.'

He started the car, then stalled it through being nervous.

'Sorry Sir.'

'Take your time lad' I said, 'who's your CO?'

'Captain Cormack Sir.'

'Right, I'll have a word with him in the morning, you'll be excused all duties tomorrow.'

'Thank you Sir.'

You're nervous driving a Lt. Col? I thought to myself, *what about me? I've come to rob the place!*

We pulled in by a camp phone box - just a phone on a pole with a shield over it to protect it from the rain - and I rang the HQ office. 'Colonel Maitland speaking, put the duty guard officer on the line at once.'

'Yes Sir.'

I heard the voice say 'Captain, there's a Colonel Maitland on the line for you.'

Peter came to the phone and we spoke in a pre-arranged code that told me 'Yes, all's well, go ahead with our plan.'

As we pulled up outside the office, the men were lined up ready for inspection. I marched quickly along the rank looking them up and down, this was no time to pick fault, so I turned to Peter and said 'Splendid turn out Captain, good body of men.'

Peter said 'Thank you Sir.'

'Right Corporal, dismiss the men and back on guard.'

Those standing nearby could overhear us, so I continued, 'I'm Maitland and you are?'

'Captain Hill Sir.'

'Right Hill, as I explained on the phone, there has been some sort of stupid cock-up at the pay office. You know what the pay corps are like, the money you have here is meant to be for A, B.and C companies. I have HQ's in the staff car, so we'll change over and I'll take it to them. Has the tea wagon been yet?'

'Yes Sir, it came about half hour ago.'

I knew it had of course, but said 'Well done, splendid, I'll have a cup then as I've been driving around half the bloody night because of these idiots.'

Peter snapped 'Corporal, a cup of tea for the Colonel.'

'Yes Sir'

And get two men to bring the cases out of the staff car and put these ones in at the double.'

'Yes Sir.'

As I drank the welcome tea, I realised my hand was now thankfully dead- steady.

Peter who looked dreadful, far too dreadful to be acting, then sank into a chair. He was shaking like a leaf and sweating buckets.

'I say Old Chap, are you alright?'

'Not too good Sir, attack of the dreaded Malaria'

With that, he rolled off the chair onto the floor and started being violently sick.

'Corporal, phone the medical centre and get them down here pronto! No, wait cancel that, they will take too long to get here, get my driver in here. Do you have a car captain?'

'Yes', he said, with his eyes rolling, 'the Austin outside.'

'Right, give me the keys old chap.'

He fished in his pockets and handed them to me, his hands shaking uncontrollably.

'Right, driver, I want you to take Captain Hill to the medical centre at top speed in his car as he's in a bad way. Get a couple of blankets and keep him warm. Now I want four men to get him into the car and two men to go with him to help you Corporal. When you get there, stay with him until you're dismissed. Do you understand?'

'Yes Sir.'

'Right, at the double.'

'Yes Sir.'

Then to the guard Corporal I said, 'I'll take the cases in the staff car to the guard room by the camp entrance, they are regimental police and can take them on to A.B and C companies for me. I'll get back here as soon as possible but there may be a delay, so take over the guard duty, and until then Corporal you are in command. Understood?'

He saluted and yelled 'Yes Sir!' Peter's car roared away and I followed in the Humber, they turned off for the medical centre and I headed for the camp entrance.

It looked like the same soldier was still on duty, but to my horror, the barrier was now down. A search of the car was the last thing on earth I wanted, so I lowered the window, stuck my head out and yelled 'Raise the barrier, Colonel Maitland on my way to Ambrosden, urgent.'

Ambrosden was an army housing estate a couple of miles away where married army personnel lived with their families. He ran over and raised the barrier, and of course saluted. I was on my way.

Back on the main road I pulled over, took off all the car's army badges, put the raincoat and trilby back on and my foot down hard. It was a clear night, the Humber wasn't a fast car, but I made good time averaging 60 mph until I hit the London suburbs, and made it back to my place just before 7am where I dumped the cases and got out of uniform. While the traffic was still light I drove the Humber way up to Hendon in north London, parked it in a quiet side street and caught the tube back to Oxford circus. I was in Hendon on business about 5 months later, and the Humber was still there, looking dirty and weather-beaten, probably still there today!

The cases each had a strong padlock that took some breaking with powerful bolt croppers. But, once opened, there it all was - pack upon pack of wage envelopes' plus wads of cash in bundles from the NAAFI club, the Globe cinema, Officers and Sergeants mess takings, and so on and lovely so on! The total came to around £80,000, none of it in brand new notes as we had feared. Something Peter had not bargained for was that over £2,000 of it was in foreign currency (German, and Cypriot). As we had troops stationed there it must have been something to do with that. I carried out Peter's orders and burnt all the foreign notes in my open fireplace along with about £1,000 in cheques, and other documents and paperwork.

It's a very strange feeling burning money. My Colonel's uniform, shirt, and tie also went up in smoke. My share was well over £33,000. Allowing for a yearly inflation rate of say 2%, that 33 grand in '62 would be worth close-on £530,000 today. I slowly filtered it into my accounts via my various businesses. I bought

Mary a nice flat in Lambeth and put money in trust for the girls. So I was home and dry.

But Peter had to take some real heavy shit. He was given some nasty grilling by the Military Police and he was put up for a court martial but it never happened. He was busted down in rank back to his old 2nd Lieutenant for incompetence and discharged after 4 hard months on medical grounds. What stood him in good stead was his excellent record fighting abroad, getting wounded, and the fact that he was so ill that night with Malaria. All the other men involved were given one month's CB (Confined to Barracks), I assume for not spotting that the Lt Col was a fake.

The civilian police were never called in and there was never a word about it in the press. Peter said years later that there must have been a *D notice* put on the whole business. The army always close ranks at any hint of trouble and all problems are dealt with in-house. The military also have a strong dislike of the civilian police, who they laughingly describe as plastic soldiers.

Peter had a brother with a small hotel in the Isle of Man. He went to work with him, and then with the help of his share of the money, they moved to the Isle of Wight and bought a bigger place. He waited over two years before he took his entire share, in case he was being watched. We kept in touch by phone and had one meeting a couple of years after the event in Soho Square on a summer's day. I sat on a seat reading *The Times*, then Peter sat next to me.

'Do we need all this cloak and dagger stuff? Can't we go and have a meal somewhere?' I asked from behind the big pages of the paper.

'Mustn't get careless Old Sport,' he said, laughing behind a hanky held to his mouth like he had a bad cold. 'You were bloody brilliant Jimmy. You know you're young driver? When he gave evidence he said; 'That man must at some time have been a high ranking officer in the army because he was every inch a Colonel.'

'Praise indeed Peter, and what about you? I thought you were dying, all that rolling on the floor and throwing up all over my new uniform.'

'That wasn't acting Old Sport; I've never felt so bloody ill in my life.'

'The most important point is Peter, we made it.' I said. 'We pulled it off because we had the nerve and the guts, and now we'll never be really poor again, so you can go and buy that Bentley.'

'Gone one better Old Sport, I have a Roller, she's ten years old and my pride and joy.'

'I'm surprised you didn't buy a new one Peter.'

He laughed. 'No, mustn't get careless Old Sport, so I've put it in my brother's name.'

'Very wise Peter, I've got mine down as owned by 'Soho Cars,' but I won't sell it, I love driving around in it too much.'

'Hold on, Old Sport, what are we talking about?'

'We're talking about my Rolls Royce.'

He gave me a puzzled look then threw his head back laughing and said 'I thought we were going to keep a low profile after the robbery.'

'Fuck low profiles, we are in the clear, the army have written it off as a loss ages ago. Come on, I'll take you for a spin, it's parked on the other side of the square.'

When we got there, he stood looking at it like an art lover gazing at the Mona Lisa, then said 'Tell me about it.'

'She's a 1930 model, only 60,000 on the clock and the last owner was a Duke. It was black but the duke changed that. As you can see his favourite colour was yellow.' I handed him the keys and said 'Let's go down to Hyde Park and get a bite.'

He drove it like a new Father taking his newborn baby out in a pram.

'So, you're a car nut like me Jimmy? I remember when you had an old American motor bike.'

'Yeah, you had an Alvis, and the bike wasn't mine, it belonged to a pal. Now we both have Rollers so we've gotta be doing something right.'

We sat in the back of the car drinking our tea in grand style off the highly polished tables that fold down from the front seats, going over details of our master-crime and some finer points about moving the money around. As I drove him back he said 'Come over and I'll take you round the Island in mine. I'll even let you drive it.'

Sadly I never did but I kept that lovely old car for over 20 years. I had a lockup over in Mayfair and when I sold that and the car together in the 1990s they pulled in just over a million. A good garage in the West End today will fetch a couple of million plus, they're like gold-dust.

Peter developed emphysema and died in his early 50s. He was a great guy and I think that under his calm, elegant, gentlemanly *David Niven* style, he was a wild gambler, and a very good one.

Chapter 15 - I Delight In Robbing The Government

Soho Cars was on its last legs. Sales were down to about one a month, people started to want a guarantee, plus after-sales service, which of course I couldn't give, so I closed it down. But on the advice of my accountant, I kept it open on the books as a tax loss. Unable to live a crime-free life, I luckily came up with a nice little scam, This and all my future crimes were down to sheer greed or maybe the excitement and thrill it gave me, because thanks to the *Army*, I was now very well off. I always took a special delight in robbing the Government.

The very charming guy who lived upstairs with his wife and three small kids, was, I assumed an Indian, but when talking one day he told me he was from Ceylon (now called Sri Lanka). He would go up North for weeks at a time to visit relatives in Birmingham. Then one day I got a long, very sad letter from his wife to say he had died up there, and she was taking the children and returning to Ceylon, so could I help by packing their few personal possessions and sending them to a Ceylon address. And could I also sell their furniture? I did this, sent her the money and told her not to worry about costs or any rent that was due. I felt I owed them for being such nice tenants.

A couple of weeks later, a new passport arrived for him, he must have sent for one just prior to his death. I intended to send it back with a note explaining, but put it in my desk drawer, got delayed by something and forgot about it. One evening a month or two later, working at my desk with my usual glass of sweet sherry, I came across it again and realised I knew all about my late tenant. The ages and names of his wife and kids, his last address, his last job and so on ...and above all his National Insurance number.

So I decided to take on his identity. His name was Patrick DeSilver. This was an advantage as I don't look Indian, and this was not, to me, an Indian or Ceylon sounding name. I sent for his birth certificate, and received a closing bank statement and cheque from the National Westminster (now called NatWest). He had about £240 in his account so I sent this on to his wife. I now knew what bank to avoid. To walk into his bank and try and set up an account in his name would have been fatal. He didn't drive so I applied for a driving test in his name over in Paddington and passed first time. I now had his driving licence.

I went over to Bloomsbury to open a bank account and started it off with £250. That may sound modest, but remember the average weekly wage was then only around £45. Of course they wanted to see my Birth certificate, Driving Licence, and Passport, all of which I handed over the counter. The nosy clerk asked 'Why bank right over here when you live in Soho?' I gave him a silly story about my very ill Father living close by who I came over to nurse almost every day. He suddenly went all kindly and humble, sickly humble, saying 'Yes yes I quite understand.' I thought *no you don't you little prick, if you did you'd take great delight in phoning the police!*

I then went to the labour exchange and signed on as unemployed and drew unemployment benefit that included money for my wife and kids, plus of course, my rent. The whole lot came to (in today's money) over two grand a month. Nice one. Me One, Government Nil. Every week I would travel over to the Post Office in Holborn dressed in old jeans and scruffy coat, collect the cash, walk around the corner, make sure I wasn't being followed, then grab a cab back to Soho. After a few weeks they wrote asking if I had a bank account so it could be paid direct into that account, and as I now did have one, that was that. Every 6 or 7 weeks I would call at the bank and withdraw a very useful big wad of cash.

I used the now empty flat upstairs myself, after all I was being paid rent for it. My girls came over a lot, sometimes with Mary, and stayed the night. They loved London and were growing up fast so they would take themselves shopping in Regent Street or go and see some pop star at the Palladium. I loved seeing them enjoy their young life in the swinging London of that time. Especially when I looked back on young life in my time – war, death, poverty and destruction all round - and later, the army.

My accountant told me about a lovely little 4 bedroom terraced house in nearby Marshall Street. The seller needed money quick and it was going for £5,000 freehold to a cash buyer. That was £1,000 under market value; I went for it, a real cosy place. I then put 11a Newburgh up for rent. But of course I had to stop claiming housing benefit for Pat DeSilver as to do so would have been too risky. But I'd had a very nice run of money out of it. All told it must have come to over £30,000.

One afternoon, while working in my front room office at my new place in Marshall Street, a woman called and introduced herself as Teresa (her surname was an unpronounceable French one). She was about 35, blonde smartly dressed, attractive with a strong, sexy French accent.

Remembering her now, she was a lookalike for modern day film actress Laura Vandervoort. She sat opposite me crossing her shapely legs; the mini skirt had just come into fashion. Then lighting a French cigarette she said. My 'usband and I would like to rent your 'ouse in Newburgh Street. We publish magazines so we would work from there.'

I pointed out that the lease states it's for residential not commercial use but if she was writing or typing in there, who the hell would know? So, OK. She offered to pay 3 months in advance. My old lady on the top floor had by then gone into a home after sadly suffering a stroke, so the place was empty.

Chapter 16 - Carnaby Street And The Swinging 60s

Looking back, my greed overcame my caution. I showed Teresa all over the building and handed her the keys. Around that same time I made a colossal business mistake, instead of now being a multi millionaire I could have been a billionaire. I knew John Stephens, the founder of Carnaby Street, quite well. He was a Scot and very *gay*. He started one Boutique (nobody had ever heard of that word until then), then another and another and he bought up property all along the street. I would often have a chat with him in the White Horse pub at the end of Newburgh Street. Even today I still pop in there from time to time.

He knew I had been a tailor and wanted me to go in with him to bring out a range of smart, colourful, modern menswear. He hated the drab dull dark blue and grey of men's clothes of that time. But idiot that I was I politely turned him down. I thought casual wear and Carnaby Street were a passing fad and would die out within a year or so. How wrong can you be? It went on to link up with the Beatles, the Stones, Twiggy and later Flower Power. It revolutionised attitudes in Britain forever, not only in fashion and music, but in people's outlook and attitude and raged on all through the 60s and 70s, making fortunes for all involved, but not me!

It didn't make much happiness for poor John though, he went completely OTT. Got a flat in Mayfair, an open-top Rolls, and could be seen driving around with his two pet Afghan dogs sitting in the back. Always very highly strung, he had a complete breakdown; the last time we spoke he was totally paranoid and convinced that people were planning to shoot him. He went back to Scotland a very wealthy but broken man.

Soho was full of fascinating characters and another one I often chatted to was Quentin Crisp (famous for his book and film "The

Naked Civil Servant"). He was of course a gay icon, even in the 1950s when men wore drab three piece suits, he went around in a wide fedora hat, long gold coat, complete with makeup and painted nails. I last saw him around 1980 when he was off to New York to live. 'I've had it with lovely old Soho, Jimmy dear boy' he said sadly. He gave me tickets for his one man show in London, it was a sell out and he was brilliant. He was highly intelligent and the best raconteur ever. I recall one of the last things he ever said to me. He was saying he had been a rent boy during the war. I said, 'Why Quentin? You're better than that.'

He replied 'I was looking for love, dear boy but all I found was degradation.'

The owner of the White Horse Pub was a retired cop, a guy called Walter Sandison. He had been a Detective Sergeant at west end central. I was alone there having a quiet drink and a snack one evening when he brought over his drink and sat with me. We chatted away but I could tell something was on his mind. 'You're sailing very close to the wind Jim, the lads over in Savile Row are checking on you.' He didn't mean tailors, he meant Police, the CID in West End central Savile Row police station. About ten things he could be referring to went through my mind, but I thought, stay calm, don't give any hint of panic. He went on 'If they prove you're living off immoral earnings you'll go away for 5 years.'

I relaxed and started to laugh. 'You had me going there for a minute Walter.' His expression stayed very serious, then he said 'You're putting on a good act, I'll say that, but not good enough to fool CID' (Criminal Investigation Department).

'OK, I'll buy it, what the hell are you talking about Walt?'

'You really don't know do you Jim? Look I get to hear a lot of things when I'm serving drinks at the bar, that French tart in your old place in Newburgh Street, is on the game, she's a pro.'

My mind went blank then I said 'You're not serious Walt?'

'Yes I am, if you go past and the street door is open, she is open for business and if the door's shut, she's not.'

I remembered that once you were past the street door you went along a short passage to a couple of steps and were then faced with another street door.

'How long before your old work mates come calling on me?' I asked.

'I'd say a couple of weeks, probably less, and they won't take *I knew nothing about it* for an excuse.'

'How the hell do her customers know she's there?'

Walt laughed, and said 'You should get around more Jim, she advertises, puts her phone number on the notice boards outside newsagents and also in these new contact magazines, that are on sale everywhere.'

'What the hell are they? Don't tell me, I don't have the time. I'm going round there now to tell her to pack her bags.'

Walter looked over at the bar, saying 'I've gotta go, there's people waiting to be served, finish your drink and stay cool as she knows you can't sling her out that easy, not without a legal fight that you will lose and it will cost you plenty. You should check out would-be tenants more carefully Jim, let me know how you get on.'

Chapter 17 - As Long As They Don't Frighten The Horses

I stepped out into the evening rain and walked quickly the few hundred yards round to 11a. The street door was open, so I walked through the short corridor and pressed the bell on the second door. A young woman opened the door, 'Do you have an appointment?' she asked.

'No, I own the building, I'm the landlord and I want to see Teresa right now, it's urgent.'

She closed the door and I heard voices, then Teresa came to the door. For a second she looked surprised, then in her heavy French accent said 'Come in Darling, nice to see you.' Once in her sitting room I cut to the chase.

'You didn't tell me what you had in mind when you took on this place; you're using it for prostitution.'

Her manner was cool and collected as she poured two whiskies. 'No ice in mine thanks.' What the hell was I doing accepting a drink? I'd come round to throw her out.

She handed me the whisky saying 'I was going to give you ice to cool you down, you are all cross with me, no? Because I charge men for sex, you dislike me very much, yes?'

'No' I replied. 'Let me tell you a story about our Queen Victoria, you've heard of her?'

'Of course, I know lot about English history.'

'OK, one day the Queen was mad, in a real temper; where's my favourite butler and maid? She demanded. 'Well your majesty', said one of her staff, 'last night, the two of them were caught in bed together, so they have both been dismissed.' 'Reinstate them at once' shouted the Queen, 'they are two of my favourite servants. 'But your Majesty....' 'Don't dare argue with me,' she yelled 'I don't care about them being in bed, in fact I don't give a damn what they get up to as long as they don't do it in the street and frighten the horses!'

Teresa fell on her settee laughing 'Ah you funny man like Maurice Chevalier!'

'No, I'm nothing like him, he's a fat old man. You see I don't judge people, I'm not a moralist but I have two daughters and I don't want them reading about their father being arrested for renting property to prostitutes.'

'You're being a silly boy, that won't 'appen, anyway there are hundreds of pros in Soho.'

'Yes', I said, most of them in property owned by the Duke of Westminster Estates or the Church of England estates. The two biggest property owners in the West End. This is the only place I have, and I want ordinary, trouble-free tenants.'

'I tell you what;' she said, getting up from her chair looking stunning, coming over to mine and leaning over me, her perfume was making my head spin. 'You come and see me now and then and there will be no charge, you like that?' For a second or so I was tempted. But my business brain kicked in.

'No,' I said, 'because I don't mix business with pleasure, and apart from that, when the police call as they are planning to do, if I accepted that offer I'd be in even more trouble.'

'OK dar-ling we leave the rent the same as it is in rent book but 'how you say, on the silent, yes?'

'I think you mean on the quiet.'

'Yes, yes, on the quiet, I give you an extra £5 a week.'

'Thanks but no thanks, please find somewhere else.'

'No, I like it here, I have a contract and I stay. Also the nasty police can't move me, 'how can they prove what a man visits me for.'

OK, she knew the rules, I was on the ropes.

I went back to the pub, Walter was busy, so I ordered a drink and found a quiet seat'. Later Walt came over. 'How did you get on? She's one gorgeous bird right?'

It dawned on me that Walt knew Teresa better than he was saying, but OK, that's his business, what the hell do I care what he does in his spare time? I told him about Teresa staying put.

'Right, first thing tomorrow, put that place in the hands of an agency. They will deal with her, you stay right out of it, also tell them you want to sell it as it is with a sitting tenant.'

'But Walt, I don't want to sell it, that's my investment for the future.'

'You're letting the grass grow under your feet Jim. Use the money you get to buy something else even if it's out in the suburbs. Property is the future; I own three flats in West London. Walter was ahead of his time, nobody could foresee the unbelievably massive rise in property prices that lay in the future. 11a that I paid £5,000 for, would set you back £2 million today - and the lease now is a very short one - or over £6,000 a month if rented. Insane or what?

Chapter 18 - Teresa, Susan, Rusty And Other Strange And Sexy Women

I had the place up for sale for several weeks but no takers. Teresa being there as a sitting tenant was definitely no help. Then Walter told me that her teenage son had been badly hurt in a motorbike accident in Paris and she was bringing him to London for medical treatment. This, I assumed would put a stop to her working there. A little later she asked me to call round, under that sexy accent and the flirting; she was one very hard-headed business woman. 'I am making big changes to my life; I make London my 'ome now, so 'ow much you want for this place?'

'I'll take 5,000', I told her.

You English highwayman, I check and know you only pay 4,000. So Dar-ling, I give you £1,500.'

I lost it... 'You thieving cow!' I got up to leave.

'You very nasty man, you call me animal names, but I don't mind' she laughed, cows are nice friendly animals. My final offer I give you £1600 cash. Don't forget you had 3 month's rent in advance.'

'That', I told her, 'is used up and you now owe rent.'

I sat down again trying to clear my head, she had me beat. So like I was told in army training, if you can't win, collect your wounded and retreat with the least damage you can.

'OK, for Christ's sake it's a deal, and I'll have another whisky.'

Thank you Dar-ling, bring your agent 'ere tomorrow and we sign papers,' she said still laughing. Getting the place for that price she had plenty to laugh about. But at least I was out of it, my girls would not be reading about their Dad in the papers.

'That's the last time I deal with so-called publishers.'

'Ah no', she laughed, 'that not big lie let me show you.' She opened a huge cupboard that, when I lived there, I stored all our clothes in.

It was packed with magazines, all taped up in blocks like they had just come from the printers. 'My 'usband was going to get into this business but we are now too busy with other things.' I didn't dare ask what those things were. 'They are nuisance to me, I store them for lady who is how you say, editor, she don't 'ave much room. She pays me £5 a week, but I need space now so I throw them in street.'

'Don't do that' I said, 'I'll take them out of here tonight and she can pay me.'

'Yes yes that's good, I tell her you hav' them. You see I rob you with 'ouse then I give you money back,' she started laughing again, and that was beginning to irritate me so I left. I sent the two lads from next door round to collect the mags and stored them in my back room. Little did I realise these mags would make up fifty-fold for my property losses with sexy Teresa in no time.

Two days later, two smart young women called on me - Susan Land and Laura Kent. 'Thank you for holding our magazines, maybe we can do business?' asked Susan, who seemed to be the main negotiator.

'How did you know Teresa?' I asked, treading carefully. 'Walter, the landlord in the White Horse introduced us.'

Walter again, I thought to myself. 'Do you know much about her?' I asked.

'You mean, do I know she's a prostitute? Of course, she advertises in our magazine.'

Warning bells were starting to ring in my head. And that was long before I had tinnitus. Laura took a copy of the mag out of her bag and handed it to me. It was A5 size, rather cheaply produced, with at that time a massive cover price of £5. Susan sat next to me explaining each page as she turned it. 'Do you know about these mags?'

'No, nothing whatsoever, I must have led a sheltered life.'

'It's called a contact magazine, because like-minded adults can contact each other.'

'What're they like minded about?' I asked.

'Sex!' they both answered at the same time, 'It's called 'Superbitch' and as you see, on each page, there are sexy photos of various ladies. I thought the mag was about as sexy as last week's Financial Times, and compared with today's standards very tame. 'We sell in all the sexy bookshops that are springing up everywhere in Soho. The shops give us about a £1 a copy, that covers our printing costs.'

'So those greedy sods are making about £4 a copy?' I replied.

'Yes, each shop takes anything from 50 to a 100 copies. We have a print run of maybe 1500 copies.'

'All very interesting Susan, but where's the profit?'

'In the letters you see, if you bought the mag and wanted to contact a lady,or ten of the ladies.'

'I don't think I'll be doing that thanks all the same.'

They both laughed. Well you're an exception, because we are getting over 4000 replies each issue. The reader can send in one letter for £1 or five letters for £4. Some send in 50 or more letters, and they have to enclose a blank stamped envelope for each letter.'

'What for?' I asked, getting slightly dazed by all this.

'So we can send the letter on to the advertiser.'

'Does it come out every week?'

'No, no, it should be every month but this is only our 2nd issue in over four months'

'Well, to me it looks like it could be a real money spinner, but I get the impression it's not being run to anywhere near its full potential.'

'Yes absolutely, so come in with us' she said matter of factly.

'Me? No thanks, I've just got out of the sex business.' I explained briefly about Teresa and my ex property. 'Also, I find it a bit of a sordid business to be in.'

'You won't be in the sex business, you'll be in publishing.'

'Why do you think you need me?'

'You come highly recommended by Teresa, and more importantly Walter.'

'You say Teresa is advertising?' Susan flicked through the pages then showed me a picture of Teresa looking very sexy in stockings, high heels and not much else, with a long advert saying how she wanted to meet exciting men - not to mention wealthy, I thought to myself. There was a box number and the location said London.

There was a section with reader's letters and a couple of articles, plus some advertising for sex shops, clubs and so on. Laura said she had to be somewhere and got up to leave, she politely shook hands saying 'I hope you join us' and took off. Susan then told me that Laura wasn't much to do with the mag, she just wrote the erotic articles. I saw little of her after that meeting.

Susan, returning to the business in hand, said 'Look Jim, I can produce the mag typed up and ready for the printer (there were no computers or discs back then), the printer is in Nottingham and, when the mag is ready, I meet him at Scratchwood, the first service station at the London end of the M1. Then, for several days, I tramp round the bookshops in Soho with a heavy bag full of mags and I go to a couple in Earls Court and Paddington, selling them, and collecting any sale or returns, not that I get many of them. And of course the idiots in the shops think they can rip me off and start getting all macho because they are dealing with a woman.'

'So where do I come in?'

'OK, I produce the mag, you deal with everything else; the shops, the printers the distributors, you're the front man. For that you get 45%, plus you know Soho backwards and have a car and I don't drive.'

'So are we partners? Where do you do the work? Do you have an office?'

'I've just moved into a larger flat in Maple Street over in Fitzrovia, North Soho.'

'Isn't that the street where the Post Office Tower is?'

'That's it, number 50.'

'Right, give me your list of shops and I'll start the rounds with this latest issue later this week. Now we'll load these mags in my car and I'll drop you off at your place.'

For a day or so I just thought about it and called on a couple of book-shops to see the type of mag the opposition were turning out. I wasn't impressed. I told Susan to stop using her real address in the mag and so cut out any nut-case callers, and fixed up an accommodation address at 19 Newport Court down in Chinatown off Gerrard Street. Run by a guy I knew called Barny, it was a small kiosk selling sweets, cigarettes, magazines and of course taking in letters. You could, for around £10 a month, set up an address and have all your mail sent there. Barny would send it on to you, or in our case Maple Street, or I'd call in every few days and collect. That became the mags HQ. and I started to ask around about this new business I found myself in.

Through Walter and some other contacts, I learnt that a certain Jimmy Humphreys and his wife Rusty were the big wheels in this business that was pulling in millions a year. The sexy bookshops were open from 10am to midnight seven days a week, stacked with books, magazines and later videos of a sexual content. I found that the biggest shop was called *Ram Books* in Old Compton street run by a tough front man called Cliff Freasy. Through him I fixed a meeting with Humphreys. Him and his wife had a flat in Dean Street. His white Rolls was parked outside, always a good sign - remember, there were no parking meters or yellow lines back then.

Chapter 19 - Bribes And Corruption

Humphreys was smartly dressed, good looking, quietly spoken and very polite. But my sixth-sense told me he could be very dangerous. I told him all about *Superbitch*, it was small-time but better than all the other like mags I'd seen - maybe because women ran it. We didn't want to tread on any toes, so I suggested we work together. 'This is my idea' I told him as Rusty handed me a drink. Just for the record, dear reader, she was not young but very attractive, had been a stripper and her stage name was Rusty Gaynor. With a name like Rusty, she was of course, a redhead.

I found it hard to keep my eyes off her. 'That shop you have Jim, *Ram Books*, you have around forty branches in Soho?'

'That's correct' he said 'OK, so say I deal only and totally with you. We no longer sell our mag to anyone else. No other shop gets a copy, no more sending to shops in the Midlands or up North but we do keep the mail order side and our subscription customers. How many can you move in your shops?'

He was starting to look pleased and more importantly interested. 'I would say 8,000 in 6 or 7 weeks'. It costs me £1.2s a copy to print.

Before I asked, he said 'I'll give you a £1 a copy.'

I thought, so we lose 2 shillings a copy, but worth it to get our hands on the letter money. Also I can renegotiate the printing cost and cut out this rip off guy in Nottingham. I'd been told about a good printer in Whitechapel in the East End who would turn them out for around 15 shillings each (75p). So, much nearer and cheaper, then we'll be making 5 shillings a copy. Jim and I shook hands on it;

Rusty said 'Stay and have another drink.'

The next day I handed over that entire issue of 3000 copies to Cliff at Ram Books and he got them out to all the branches. Within a month my share was coming to around £200 a week tax free, when the average weekly wage at the time was now around £45 a week. I would call at the office two or three days a week to help Susan with re-addressing stacks of letters. Old Barny at Newport Court, every three or so days, would pack all the mail into a couple of big sacks, put them in a cab and send them up to Maple Street.

I already had a bank account in De Silver's name so it was simple to add a business account. I dealt with all the cheques, cash and general business. Susan was a strange one and I never really got to know her well. There appeared to be no-one in her life, and if you asked too many questions she would clam up. She was a brilliant ideas person, working late into the night getting the mag ready, designing the front-cover, sorting the adverts, reader's letters, and then she had ideas for other pin up type mags, so we produced them. I took them along to Jim, but Rusty now ran that side of his vast business empire.

So I worked closely with her. She was attractive company and great fun to be with, and although tempted, it didn't develop into a full blown affair. Just as well, because some years later, she did have an affair with a man well known in Soho called Peter Garfath. John heard about it, tracked him down to a nightclub and with the help of his bodyguards, beat him to a pulp then slashed him with a knife. For that he got eight years in Dartmoor but decided to turn Queens's evidence against all the cops who he felt had let him down after taking his money in bribes for many years. Eventually, 74 were arrested, 28 sacked, 13 went to prison, and Humphreys was given a Royal pardon and released after less than 2 years.

One afternoon, plain-clothes police turned up at Maple Street. We had just taken delivery of the latest issue from the printer. In the last six months I had boosted circulation to 10,000 and that's how many copies the police seized. They warned me and Susan that we would be charged with publishing obscene material. It might have been sexy but never obscene.

I called on Rusty and told her why I couldn't deliver. She phoned Jim, I could hear his voice on the other end and he sounded furious. Putting the phone down, Rusty said 'Give me a couple of hundred quid and we will straighten this out.' And they did, the next day a plain van brought the mags back and we heard no more about it. It later transpired that most of the police were taking bribes to turn a blind eye to his various business enterprises.

Unlike me, he and many other West End crooks like him; Bernie Silver, John Mason etc. never learn to back off. They start to believe their own publicity and think they're untouchable. Some years later, the whole lot came crashing down around their ears. Jim made the stupid mistake of taking a holiday in Tenerife with Police Commander Kenneth Drury, the head of Scotland Yard's Obscene Publications Squad and their wives. It cost Drury nothing, all expenses paid by Jim. The press were tipped off and it became front page news.

The upshot was trials that went on for years, The Government set up *Operation Countryman* to investigate corruption in the Soho police. It went on for 5 years and recommended that over 300 hundred police officers should be charged with taking bribes. The crooked London lawyers made millions but no police officer was ever convicted. Sixty police were got rid of, many retired on health grounds with a very nice pension, while many others resigned. Some years later when Sir Robert Mark took over as top cop, a lot of high ranking police went to prison, including Kenneth Drury who was sentenced to 7 years.

I was told by those who knew the behind-the-scenes details that what kept Drury safe for so long was that he was a high ranking freemason. But long before all that, I learned that my friend, ex-cop Walter who ran the White Horse pub, was a close pal of Billy Hill, known as *the Godfather of Soho* who even John Humphreys was careful not to cross. This was starting to remind me of my time with Laura and the East End mob she ran with. This was different, but starting to look and feel very similar. I started to feel uneasy.

What clinched it for me was, one afternoon when I called in at the White Horse for a quiet snack and a sherry. It wasn't very busy and Walt joined me for a chat. Oddly enough he was a fan of and expert on old movies going back to the silent days. He had pictures of Rudolf Valentino and Charlie Chaplin above the bar. I too liked these old films and growing up during the war was one of the cinema generation, so could chat with him in-depth on the subject. After covering Hollywood in the 1920's at some length, he asked how the magazine business was going. I brought him up to date, and that I was now getting over £400 a week out of it.

I told him I was very pleased for his help with Teresa and sending Susan Land my way, I owed him. He protested of course: *What are friends for?* and so on. Then he said 'I've heard on the grapevine that the only danger you and Susan face is they could have you for living off immoral earnings.'

'No Walt, I got out of that, you're thinking of Teresa round at No.11a.'

'No no' he said, lowering his voice. 'If one of those women advertising in the mag is a pro, and most of them are, and you're charging an advertising fee, then you're accepting money from her.'

'Come on Walt', I replied 'if the same woman came in and ordered a drink, then so are you.'

'Yeah, but I don't know what she does for a living, whereas you do. It's a grey area Jim, so be careful.'

Later, I thought hard about it, phoned Susan and told her that in all future issues, women advertised free. But the die was cast, my sixth-sense was telling me to pull out. Over-cautious, too jumpy maybe, but that's how I've stayed safe all these years. Since I joined up with Susan I'd built the mag up, got it on a firm footing and quadrupled the circulation. This in turn meant we were pulling in around 550 letters a day, working out at around £650 a day. Susan was cross that I wanted to pull out, but I set her up with a likeable guy I met in the business, Ron Dawson. He ran five similar mags over in Essex, where he lived in a house with a swimming pool.

Susan's argument was - surely for this money it's worth getting nicked now and then, paying a fine and pressing on? But I wanted at all costs to keep my clean record. So I was out, I'd recouped the money I lost on the Newburgh Street property multiplied by about 100. I wasn't mega-rich but I was very comfortable, for the time being at least.

Susan and Ron went on to produce a whole range of magazines, and later blue videos. That was their downfall, they both got nicked and got six months each, but came out after three and carried on like nothing had changed, but it had.

There was a new top cop in charge of the West End police; Sir Robert Mark. He was out to wipe out the sexy bookshops, strip clubs, peep show booths, brothels and clean up Soho as it was fast running out of control. He also aimed to target all the police who had turned a blind eye and taken bribes.

Ron Dawson, who in his heyday had a Rolls, died a few years ago and at the end he was struggling with his last magazine that he only sent out mail order, earning peanuts. The car and his house with the pool were all gone.

The last I heard about Susan, she had been set up with a new false identity and moved to America alone. No man or woman friend I knew of. If I ever asked even a remotely personal question, a glass wall would come down, so she stayed a mysterious lone wolf to the end. Funny how they all bought Rolls Royces as soon as they made big money. Not a good way to keep a low profile, like they should have been doing. I know I had one but I kept it out of sight and drove around Soho with the mags in an old VW.

I mentioned this to Cliff Freasy one day at *Ram Books*, he agreed, saying 'It's not a car I would buy, draws too much attention.' When I asked what car he drove he said, 'I've just got myself a Ferrari!'

Looking back it all seems rather pointless when you read about pornography on the modern day internet. Compared with that, our publications were mere pin-up mags. All those old-time gangsters and police must be turning in their graves.

I had one of the first credit cards in Patrick DeSilver's name, no pin numbers back then, all you had to do was sign. I asked Walter to give me his sizes for suits, shirts, etc. Got a cab to Harrods and ran up a bill of over two thousand buying him a stack of top quality clothing, and a few items for myself. It was a *Thank You* gift for all his tip-offs and good advice. Funny how DeSilver never paid his bills when debt collectors called, they were sent packing, and told he'd gone back to Ceylon, which in a way was true. Would you believe he ran up a total of over £6,000 before they put a stop on that card?

As I had nothing planned, I decided to lay low for a while and give crime, semi crime, and generally living dangerously, a rest. With my army and magazine money I did buy a 2 bed flat in Holborn and a studio flat in Bloomsbury. If you don't know London, they are places that are within walking distance of Soho and Oxford Street. I got them for £2,250 and £1,500 then put them in the hands of an agency to rent out. I sold them a year ago for £1.9 million and £1.6 million respectively to Russian businessmen.

Back then I just regarded them as little investments and a way of hiding money from the tax man. I took Mary and the girls to America for three months holiday; First Class all the way, staying at the best hotels in New York, L.A and San Francisco. Nothing special now, but regarded as the holiday of a lifetime in those days, the girls still talk about it. But as ever, Mary was unimpressed and glad to get back to Lambeth.

Chapter 20 - Moving Into The 80's

The world, and especially my world of crime and Soho, were changing rapidly and the mirror told me I was well into middle age. So time for a big rethink. I'd had a very good run over the last 30 years. First the pub in Beak Street, then the shirts from Stoke on Trent, the Mayfair tailor shop robbery, then the big one - the Army at Bicester, taking on Patrick DeSilver's identity to rob the Government, and lastly the sexy magazine business. Plus lot of little scams in between.

The money I'd made from crime enabled me to be my own man and be answerable to no one, and of course to live well. Electric and gas bills no longer worried me. When I bought a car it was a new one right out the showroom. I still had my beloved vintage Rolls that I would take for a spin in the summer and both my girls learnt to drive in it (I told them if you can drive this you can drive anything), and when one of us got ill we had private medical treatment. That's all on the plus side. But there is a flip side to that coin, it's a lonely, secretive, stressful life and you're always looking over your shoulder.

I had to be honest with myself and admit that if I carried on, it was for the excitement of seeing if I could pull it off once more. A sort of stupid pride that a lot of criminals suffer from, and of course sooner rather than later, my luck would run out. So I decided to quit, and for over a year I did nothing, dined at the best restaurants, took my dog (a descendant of dear old Major) to Hyde or Regent's Park every day and in the evening I'd get a cab down to one of the theatres in Shaftsbury Avenue and see a play. Or go to Leicester Square to see the latest movies. In the summer I would swim and sunbathe at the Oasis, which is a rooftop open-air swimming pool down in Covent Garden.

I was starting to get bored with it when I met Stella who was very attractive and 15 years younger than me. Before you say 'no fool like an old fool'; I have to tell you she was quite well off, she had come out of a very bad marriage but a wealthy one. We lived together off and on, she brought some fun into my life and we decided to go into business. She loved clothes and had worked in a Knightsbridge boutique. So we put up equal shares and opened a ladies dress shop in the Old Kent Road. After a very successful 2 years we moved to Chelsea.

Overheads there were sky-high but we still did well. At this time (rather late) I also got into the property business. But not in central London, I went for small shops with a flat above, in places that I knew in South East London, like Catford, Eltham, New Cross, and even as far down as the South coast. At one point I had 26 properties in my portfolio. Stella wanted to get married, I did not, so we started to drift apart and she bought out my share of the two boutiques. She still has the Chelsea one and is doing well. We remain friends.

Chapter 21 - The Present Day And Final Years

Some years ago, Mary asked me for a divorce. It made me sad but I agreed. She had met a man and they wanted to marry. If it made her happy, I wouldn't stand in her way. I met him, a decent guy but dull. He worked on the railway all his life but was now retired, didn't drive and never had a car. Liked nothing better than watching football on TV all evening.

We still love each other in our way, but she never wanted the West End life; she would say Soho was full of weird, dangerous people. She had a point but I always loved the place. My two girls are both married now and I have a small Grandson. I'm not keen on the men they married but I guess a lot of Dads feel that way - the *No-one's good enough for my daughter* syndrome. One son-in law's an accountant and the other a chemist. Put it this way, I could never imagine them selling stolen shirts from a stall in Berwick market.

The tragedy for me is that both girls now live in Perth, Australia. Three years ago Mary and her new husband joined them. Behind the scenes I helped Mary moneywise to settle in. I've been out there to visit three times. The girls have begged me to move out there, but no, not for me. I can't take that scorching heat and I won't make the trip again as I'm too old now for that 22 hour flight. I travel first class with all the trimmings but the last one knocked the guts out of me.

We keep in touch by phone often and on our last chat, my young Grandson Brad said 'I'm gonna come over to see yer Granddad, I want yer to show me Sohooo.'

'You bet son, but don't hang about, I ain't getting any younger.'

After saying goodbye four times, I put the phone down with tears streaming down my face, knowing of course his visit will never happen. And also knowing the Soho I love will not be around for much longer either.

It's now being massively redeveloped, bulldozers are everywhere, old interesting buildings are crashing to the ground daily to be replaced by soulless glass and concrete office blocks. The markets, the clubs, the pubs, the alleyways, the workshops, the tailors, shoemakers, jewellers, hat makers, strippers, prostitutes, gangsters, the writers, the actors, the musicians, but above all the characters. Some weird, some funny, some sexually strange, some very dangerous, the sort of people you would never meet in suburbia. But all fascinating and very interesting, alas now have almost all gone.

I've become a ghost haunting a deserted village; every street reminds me of something or someone. So that's my story of how I made crime pay. The massive rise in property made my real fortune but of course I would never have been able to get into that business without crime money to start me off. I recently sold off all my property and other assets and I'm now worth (so my account tells me) close on £10 million. That's clear, after paying tax. I've taken care of my Australian family, and the bulk of it has gone to my favourite charities. So maybe in a round-about way, some good will come of it all.

I hope you've found my story an interesting and entertaining one, and as I promised at the start, it's very different to the usual run-of-the-mill crime stories. I must now wish you well, and bid you farewell. I now sit back and await the knock on the door from either the *Almighty* or the *Old Bill*.